"SUPPORT
ONE BIBLE MISSION"

UNCOMMON
Prayers

**HELPING YOU
FIGHT LIFE'S BATTLES,
SEEK WISDOM, AND
SHOW GRATITUDE IN
ALL CIRCUMSTANCES**

MIKE BELLINI with
STEPHANIE L. JONES

Copyright © 2023 Mike Bellini and Stephanie L. Jones

All rights reserved. No part of this book may be used or reproduced by any means, graphic, electronic, or mechanical, including photocopying, recording, taping, or by any information storage-retrieval system without written permission of the author except in the case of brief quotations embodied in critical articles and reviews.

Unless otherwise noted, Scripture quotations are taken from the Holy Bible, New International Version®. Copyright © 1973, 1978, 1984, 2011 by Biblica, Inc.™ Used by permission of Zondervan. All rights reserved worldwide. www.zondervan.com. The "NIV" and "New International Version" are trademarks registered in the United States Patent and Trademark Office by Biblica, Inc.™

Scripture quotations marked (NLT) are taken from the Holy Bible, New Living Translation, copyright © 1996, 2004, 2015 by Tyndale House Foundation. Used by permission of Tyndale House Publishers, Inc., Carol Stream, Illinois 60188. All rights reserved.

Scriptures marked (KJV) are taken from the King James Version, public domain.

Scripture taken from the New King James Version®. Copyright © 1982 by Thomas Nelson. Used by permission. All rights reserved.

Quotes from President Abraham Lincoln's Thanksgiving Proclamation taken from *Harper's Weekly*, October 17, 1863.

Giving Gal Press books may be ordered by contacting Giving Gal Press, a division of Giving Gal, LLC, www.GivingGal.com, 219-707-9545.

Because of the internet's dynamic nature, any web address or links contained in this book may have changed since publication and may no longer be valid.

ISBN: 978-1-948693-23-3

Library of Congress Control Number: 2023918135

Print information is available on the last page.

Cover design by Stephanie L. Jones and Mike Bellini

Giving Gal Press Date October 1, 2023

Disclaimer and Limit of Liability

The publisher, author, and contributors have used our best efforts in preparing *Uncommon Prayers*. Other than the use of our best efforts, we make no representations or warranties concerning this book. We make no representations or warranties for the accuracy or completeness of the contents of this book. We expressly disclaim any implied warranties of merchantability or fitness for a particular purpose. No warranties may be created by implication. No oral or written statement by us or any sales representative or other third party shall make warranties. We do not guarantee or warrant the information and opinions stated in this book will produce any particular results. We caution readers that this book's advice and strategies may not be suitable for all individuals. We, individually or collectively, shall not be liable for any monetary loss, physical injury, mental anguish, property damage, loss of profit, or any other commercial, physical and emotional damages, including but not limited to special, incidental, consequential, or other damages. We, individually and/or collectively, are not engaged in rendering professional advice. If professional or psychological advice or additional expert assistance is required, a competent professional's services should be sought.

DEDICATION

Calvary Church of Valparaiso Prayer Team, thank you for accepting me into your group and diligently praying over every part and person in our church and community.

Grandma B, thank you for showing me this powerful discipline by praying for me and my family every night. It changed my life more than I knew at the time. I look forward to praying and praising together when we meet again among the heavenly host.

CONTENTS

Foreword 1
Introduction 3
Scriptural Prayers 11
Personal Prayers 39
Short Prayers 81
Intentional Prayers 101
Global Prayers 121
After Prayers 147
Bonus Prayer Moments 153
When You Don't Know What Or Who To Pray For 161
Appendix 166
Acknowledgments 169

FOREWORD

Every Sunday, Mike posts a prayer on social media. The prayers are short yet impactful. His words to our Heavenly Father bring me peace, comfort, and calmness in my spirit.

Leading up to the 2022 mid-term election, Mike boldly went live on Instagram and prayed for our families, children, politicians, educators, and first responders. His prayers were powerful, and he reminded us of the power of praying using scripture. These were not Mike's words but messages we had been given from God to help us navigate life.

On more than one occasion, I casually mentioned to Mike, "You should write a book on prayer."

I think he ignored my first nudge.

But as he consistently posted his Sunday prayers, my spirit stirred, and I again sent him a message. "I think I've asked you before, but are you going to turn your prayers into a book of prayers? I love them. Today's prayer was so good! I believe in this book so much that I'd even pay for everything and publish it. #Justsaying"

Mike quickly replied, "I really haven't thought about it much, but I would love to have the conversation."

We scheduled a time to chat, Mike prayed about pursuing this book, and as they say, the rest is history.

FOREWORD

I worked with Mike on his first book, *Ultra Marriage*, and he not only talks the talk but walks the walk in his faith, marriage, and showing up for his friends.

What I love about how this book came to be is that it highlights how God can use us to encourage others to pursue an opportunity they may not have thought of and to be obedient in going to God in prayer, seeking His guidance, and acting on His purpose for our life.

As you read through *Uncommon Prayers*, I pray that you grow in your faith and relationship with God and become a prayer warrior for friends, family, strangers, community, and country.

Blessings,

Stephanie

INTRODUCTION

"It's not good," my mother faintly said. I will never forget her voice when she called to tell me the news.

She hadn't been feeling well for a few months, and she called to tell me she had terminal cancer in an inoperable location. Clinical trials and other treatments to prolong her life were her only hope.

My mother was a short, feisty, stubborn Italian woman. She tried a few of the things doctors suggested might help, and she did many things they said she shouldn't. Aside from the medical treatments, she went to prayer gatherings for healing, asked her priest to bless her after every church service, and had countless others praying for her.

She carried on and beat a devastating disease far longer than anyone could have anticipated.

In the final stage of this battle, she visited some new doctors, searching for any last treatments that had not yet been tried. There were none. But the doctors were astonished when they learned how long she had lived with the disease. The average lifespan of a patient with her type of cancer, at the stage it was discovered, is nine to twelve months. My mother had beaten the disease for over *seven* years, on little more than trial, error, and prayer.

When the cancer was first diagnosed, her doctors immediately ruled out the prospect of surgery because they presumed recovery from the surgery would take longer

INTRODUCTION

than the amount of time before her body succumbed to cancer. So they just tried to keep her as comfortable as possible for as long as her body would respond to the treatments. Little did they know, she had another mighty brand of treatment at work. She didn't "just survive" for those seven years, either. We made memories together that can never be taken away, moments we will cherish forever.

Having watched my mother live through this as long as she did, bucking the trend and advice of her doctors, then seeing how amazed they were to learn about the successful length of her battle in the end, I'm led to one conclusion—one logical explanation as to why she was given seven times more remaining life than the average person with her disease. Prayer.

"Please pray for me." Is there a more sobering request to hear from another person? Those four simple words conjure images of desperation, situations that are entirely out of our control and, without God's intervention, outcomes that may be dire. They suggest circumstances that simply cannot be resolved except by God.

Yet, we tend to treat prayer casually. We may use prayer as a personal wish list or a last resort in troubling times. We say a prayer, then forget what we prayed, and go about our day without believing that an answer is forthcoming. Do we pray only because we think we should pray, or is there a meaningful purpose behind it all? Suppose we are doing it out of obligation only. In that case, we risk watering down our prayers so much that, when a situation worthy of a desperate prayer arises, we feel unqualified or unprepared to fervently entreat God.

Instead of waiting to approach God in prayer as a final attempt at getting help in a desperate place, what if we focused on building a relationship with Him? And as we build that relationship, we go to Him with bold, urgent, righteous prayers? The biggest question to answer is, do we believe that prayer has power and, if so, do our prayers reflect that belief?

Chances are, if you believe in God, you pray regularly or at least periodically. If you have prayed, you probably have received an answer in response. However, if you are in the habit of praying often, many prayers have undoubtedly gone unanswered. So how does it work, and why keep doing it?

Let's get the first question out of the way. How does prayer work? Truthfully, I don't exactly know. I don't know how God hears us when we pray silently or speak out loud. I don't know how He hears everyone simultaneously and answers us all. I don't know how He manifests responses from the spiritual realm into our physical existence on Earth. However, I don't need to know *how* it works to believe that it does. I don't understand how a cell phone works, but I know what it is capable of doing because I see it happen. I may not know how God answers prayers, but I have witnessed answers to prayers enough times that I know it is real and powerful. I am sure you have as well.

At a certain point in my spiritual journey, I desired to become more like Jesus. I realized that I and my life would be much better if I followed the example of John the Baptist's words in John 3:30: "'He [Jesus] must increase, but I must decrease'" (KJV).

A pathway to becoming more like Jesus is to do things that He did, to act more like Him, so that His character comes out of us more than our flawed character might. That begs the question, "What did Jesus do that we can do?" Unfortunately, there are many things He did that we cannot, at least not yet. We haven't figured out how to walk on water. We don't know how to turn water into wine. We have never raised a dead person back to life, at least not after having been dead for a couple of days. Among all the miraculous wonders Jesus performed, there is one He did frequently and quite zealously that we can do as well. He prayed.

If we embark on a mission to pray more like Jesus, we should first look at the Bible to see what He said about prayer. The disciples asked Him directly how they should pray, and from His answer we received the Lord's Prayer—a model for us to follow. Jesus went on to say in Matthew 6:7, "'When you pray, do not keep on babbling like pagans, for they think they will be heard because of their many words.'" From this, we can surmise that prayer does not have to be long. We don't need to give God the whole scenario around what and why we are praying as if trying to inform Him of what is happening. He knows. We need to tell Him what is on our heart and why we are coming to Him.

In an often-quoted verse, Matthew 7:7-8, Jesus said, "'Ask, and it will be given to you… For everyone who asks receives.'" This is true in many respects. If we, in thought, ask ourselves a question, our brain will give us an answer. It will give us a habitual answer previously recorded in our mind, a reactive answer based on our emotions at the moment, or an intuitive answer if we take the time to analyze the question diligently. Similarly, if we ask a question to another person, we will get an answer in return.

The answer may be "No" or "Don't know," but we will get one. Asking a question to ourselves or someone else will elicit an answer, whether or not it is the answer we want to hear. The first step in receiving the best possible answer in life—and in prayer—is to ask the best possible question.

Mark wrote in chapter 11, verse 24, of his book that Jesus also said, "'Whatever you ask for in prayer, believe that you have received it, and it will be yours.'" Belief is another significant component in unleashing the power of prayer. But can we ask God for anything and receive it if we just believe? Will that work if we ask for ten million dollars or our social media platform to go viral? Does God hand out wishes like a genie if we believe the wish will come true? Of course not. No parent should give their children everything they ask for, because parents have more knowledge of what would be beneficial or potentially destructive. God is infinitely more knowledgeable than us. Isaiah 55:8-9 says, "'For my thoughts are not your thoughts, neither are your ways my ways,' declares the LORD. 'As the heavens are higher than the earth, so are my ways higher than your ways and my thoughts than your thoughts.'"

How, then, do we combine a good question with belief to elicit an answer from God? John 14:13-14 gives us a clue, recording Jesus saying, "'And I will do whatever you ask in my name, so that the Father may be glorified in the Son. You may ask me for anything in my name, and I will do it.'" Therefore, what we ask of God must be *in Jesus' name*, and if it is, He will do it. Why will He do it? "So that the Father may be glorified in the Son." It won't be done for our glorification. It won't be for our benefit here on Earth, but so that Jesus is glorified on the earth, to bring more people to Him. As a result of these prayers, our ultimate benefit and prosperity will be in heaven! So ask, believe, and do it all in Jesus' name.

Does God need our prayers to release His power and accomplish His will? Perhaps not. However, the prophet Isaiah sent a message to King Hezekiah, as written in Isaiah 37:21-22, "'This is what the LORD, the God of Israel, says: Because you have prayed to me concerning Sennacherib king of Assyria, this is the word the LORD has spoken against him.'" What stands out in this passage is the statement, "Because you have prayed." It presents the notion that God would not have responded if the king had not prayed. It tells us that our prayers do matter in God's eyes.

Jesus told His disciples, "'Your Father knows what you need before you ask him'" (Matthew 6:8). If that is true, why pray at all? If God knows what we need and want, can't He just give it to us? Sometimes. Most of the time, the purpose of prayer is for *our* benefit and growth.

Whether God needs our prayers or not to unleash power from the spiritual realm, communing with Him in prayer helps us focus more on His purposes, what He is doing in our lives and in the earth. Clarity and specificity provide power. The clearer we are in creating a vision or a goal to move toward, the more likely we are to reach it or at least come close to it. Prayer works the same way. God knows the specifics of our situation. He doesn't need us to tell Him what they are or to give *Him* clarity. We need Him to give *us* clarity on our purpose, our participation in that purpose, what we need to look for, and what actions we should take next. Prayer helps us become centered with God, clearer about our own life, what we need, what God wants, and how we can better align with His will.

Let's also look at prayer from the perspective of a change we want to make in ourselves. For example, a habit or addiction which we are asking God's help to overcome.

The first step in making any kind of change is to acknowledge or admit that we need a change. However, until we reach a point of *wanting* to make that change, all efforts are futile. Without a desire to be different, we will simply revert to the same behavior without desiring a different path. Prayer is a way of saying to God, "I want this!" We may want a change, a certain result, to commune with Him, or to see Him working in our lives. God may put everything we need in our path, and we could still say "No" to His invitation. Until we say "Yes," we won't be ready to accept it. Prayer is an opportunity to say "Yes" to whatever answer God is ready to provide for what He already knows we need.

James wrote in chapter 5 verse 16 of his New Testament book "The effective, fervent prayer of a righteous man avails much" (NKJV). If we take God at His word and believe His promises, why would we *not* pray as a *first* resort in times of need?

Remember, prayer does not excuse us from acting and doing our part, but it sets us up for greater success with the power of God directing and helping us as we strive forward. This book is a guide to pray with more significance, courage, and precision. It will not help you become righteous, as James indicates is a prerequisite for prayers that accomplish much. None of us are righteous on our own. There is only One who is righteous, which is why we pray in His name. Hopefully, this book will help lead you to a more earnest prayer life. For, an effective, fervent prayer in Jesus' name can accomplish so much more than

INTRODUCTION

we could ever realize. How do I know this is true? I have seen this power many times throughout my life. Remember my mother's miraculous journey?

Prayer helps us build a relationship with God and rely on Him for all we do, in the good and bad times. We grow in our faith and become more like Jesus; our heart softens, and we learn to hear His voice and know when He is nudging us.

What we pray for and about can vary based on people and situations. We can pray for others, ourselves, individuals, organizations, or nations. We can pray for help in the moment, a health concern, a difficult circumstance, or a long-term situation. Whatever the reason, know that prayer is a discipline, no different than any other and one that should be exercised daily.

This book contains different types of prayers, written in a method that is specific, clear, and direct; that understands a situation, knows what is needed or being asked, and, ultimately, leads to knowing God more intimately. It is designed to help you pray—whether you are just now learning, starting to do it more often, or seeking to pray more fervently. It offers some direction and strategies for making your prayer experience more powerful and deepening your relationship with God. Whatever your motivation, use this book as a guide to finding your voice in talking with and appealing to the Creator of heaven and earth.

May you uncover powerful and effective prayers to accomplish the perfect loving will of Him to whom we make our requests.

SCRIPTURAL PRAYERS

Devote yourselves to prayer with an alert mind and a thankful heart.

Colossians 4:2 NLT

SCRIPTURAL PRAYERS

The Bible is filled with prayers and prayerful language. The book of Psalms, for instance, is an entire collection of prayers and conversations with God. Many other books include prayers of the writer or people being written about, most notably, the Lord's Prayer that Jesus taught His disciples.

Aside from the actual prayers in the Bible, did you know we can use scripture as prayers? There are several specific reasons to draw from scripture when we pray. First, there is power in God's Word—and not just any power. It is almighty creative power. Genesis 1:3 says, "And God said, 'Let there be light,' and there was light." Genesis 1 records nine times that God spoke and something was created. His words have command, authority, and the ability to create something from nothing.

In 2 Timothy 3:16-17, Paul wrote, "All scripture is God-breathed and is useful for teaching, rebuking, correcting and training in righteousness, so that the servant of God may be thoroughly equipped for every good work." I would include that all scripture is useful for prayer, so our prayers may also be fully equipped.

Furthermore, the prophet Isaiah wrote in Isaiah 55:11 that God says, "'So is my word that goes out from my mouth; it will not return to me empty, but will accomplish what I desire and achieve the purpose for which I sent it.'" This is what we want from our prayers, spoken from our mouths and accomplishing the purpose for which they have been said.

A second reason for using scripture is to align with God's will and gain certainty that we are asking in Jesus' name. John 14:14 recounts Jesus saying, "'You may ask for anything in my name, and I will do it.'" What does it mean to ask, "in Jesus' name," and how can we be sure to pray in that way? When we ask in His name, we want what *He* wants, not what *we* want. When we pray "in Jesus' name," we use His authority. When we speak to God, we often don't know or understand what we are asking or need. It's okay to be in that place because, ultimately, we should want what God wants in any circumstance, and we can discern a lot of what He wants from scripture. The best, most assured, way to pray in His name, or in the name of the Father, Son, and Holy Spirit, is to pray from the pages of the Bible.

Whatever we are going through, whatever we need, whatever we're asking for or committing to, there is scripture that will speak directly to it. Using scripture will give our words authority. All prayers in this book have references to certain Bible verses. After reading a prayer, look up the verses listed to identify how they are used and to start using scripture in your prayers every day.

Prayer Moment (Mike)

My wife and I had relocated to be closer to her family. We had two children under five years old and were both out of work for over a year. It was a stressful time in many respects. Eventually, I found a job with a start-up company at a salary that came close to, but didn't quite, cover our monthly expenses. When I began working there, I had the overwhelming sense that God had sent me there for a reason. It was a blessing until I found out what was really going on behind the scenes. A few months after being hired, I learned that a part-owner was committing bank fraud to acquire cash to pay overdue bills. Those actions violated a standard of behavior and code of ethics I strive to live by. With very little savings and a young family to support, we faced a significant dilemma.

My wife and I prayed... a lot.

"I brought you there, and I will take you out of there when it is time," I heard God say. So, while feverishly searching for another job, I stayed with the company to try to impact positive change. Almost every day for the next few months, I prayed Psalm 91. It was my overwhelming petition to God. I believe I had a part in this prayer... to continue seeking God and acting with integrity. In return, I trusted in His protection and guidance.

Eventually, the company reached a point of financial collapse and started shedding costs. I was one of the first casualties, mainly because I refused to do business according to their immoral practices and demands. Unfortunately, it again left our family without an income for the foreseeable future. Then God showed us how He answered our prayers, specifically from Psalm 91.

"You will not fear the terror of night, nor the arrow that flies by day," says Psalm 91:5. Somehow, though we had very little savings and were staring at the prospect of having no income right at the beginning of the housing and stock market collapse of 2007, we were at peace. It was illogical and unexplainable, except we knew this was an opportunity to put our full trust in God. Psalm 91:2 says, "I will say of the LORD, 'He is my refuge and my fortress, my God, in whom I trust.'" That was us. We may have had no other choice, but it was our choice, nonetheless.

"'Because he loves me,' says the LORD, 'I will rescue him; I will protect him, for he acknowledges my name. He will call on me, and I will answer him; I will be with him in trouble, I will deliver him and honor him'" (Psalm 91:14-15). Without question, God rescued me. He was true to the word I had heard Him speak months earlier regarding my stay at that company; when it was time, He got me out. Then, He delivered me. Two months later, I received an offer from a company I have been with for over fifteen years. He pulled me out of the pit and brought me to a place of refuge.

He also showed me what He had rescued me from. Four months after I was fired, the company I had left collapsed and was embroiled in lawsuits. "A thousand may fall at your side, ten thousand at your right hand, but it will not come near you. You will only observe with your eyes and see the punishment of the wicked" (Psalm 91:7-8). He honored that declaration. No consequence of the company's fall touched me at all. I was simply an innocent observer.

While praying Psalm 91 throughout this tumultuous season, I didn't know how God would answer. I simply trusted that He would. He is faithful to His promises. He will always be true to His word if we do our part too.

The Lord's Prayer

This is where prayer starts. When the disciples asked Jesus to teach them how to pray, He responded with what we commonly call The Lord's Prayer. It is short, to the point, and unselfish. Breaking it down, we see a few distinct intentions.

First, we greet God with acknowledgment of His holiness and sovereignty.

Second, we request our needs for the day. Notice that Jesus did not suggest we ask for what we *want*. Bread symbolizes a basic need in life, and the ask is for what we need *today*. The petition does not indicate ordering off a menu for an abundance of food to last throughout the winter. It focuses only on what we need right now. After teaching this prayer, Jesus instructed the disciples, "Do not worry about tomorrow" (Matthew 6:34). Therefore, we shouldn't be distracted by what we might need in the future. God will provide what we need when we need it. Be fully present now, focusing only on today.

Third, we seek His heavenly purpose, not ours, in any situation.

Fourth, we ask forgiveness for ourselves and grant forgiveness to others who may have wronged us. In teaching this to His disciples, Jesus said, "'for if you forgive other people when they sin against you, your heavenly Father will also forgive you. But if you do not forgive others their sins, your Father will not forgive your sins'" (Matthew 6:14-15). That is a very clear directive that we must forgive others if we expect forgiveness from God.

Fifth, we ask for His guidance. We know evil exists in the world, and God's protection and deliverance is essential. The world is full of temptation. Paul wrote to the church in Corinth that "God is faithful, he will not let you be tempted beyond what you can bear. But when you are tempted, he will also provide a way out so that you can endure it" (1 Corinthians 10:13). We pray that God leads us along a straight path. Still, when we stray, we pray for deliverance to return to Him.

Last, we declare that God's authority is supreme. Everything we ask is to be used for His purpose and His glory.

Prayer

Our Father which art in heaven,

Hallowed be thy name.

Thy kingdom come.

Thy will be done in earth, as it is in heaven.

Give us this day our daily bread.

And forgive us our debts,

As we forgive our debtors.

And lead us not into temptation,

But deliver us from evil;

For thine is the kingdom, and the power, and the glory forever.

Amen.

Scripture Reference: Matthew 6:9-13 (KJV)

Prayer of Confession

David was Israel's greatest king. God called him "a man after my own heart" (Acts 13:22 NLT). Still, David was a sinner and often asked for God's forgiveness, perhaps never more ardently than after he had been with another man's wife. The woman's husband was a soldier in David's army, and David set up that man to be killed in battle. He then took the man's wife as his own, and she became pregnant. When confronted about his sin, David pleaded to God for forgiveness and wrote Psalm 51.

We must accept that there are consequences for our actions. Acknowledging his sin, David begged God to be lenient with him. But, as retribution for his actions, the child born from his adulterous relationship did not survive. However, God is merciful and forgiving. David kept the woman as his wife, and they had another child. By grace, God exalted this child, Solomon, as the heir to the throne of Israel. He succeeded David as Israel's next king, and God anointed him with wisdom all his days.

God is graceful but just. He is stern but forgiving. Nothing we do is hidden from Him. Acknowledging our sins before Him is a powerful step on the road to redemption. Remember, no sin is too far from the grace of God. He welcomes us with open arms, but we must take the first step.

Prayer

Have mercy on me, O God,
according to your unfailing love;
according to your great compassion
blot out my transgressions.
Wash away all my iniquity
and cleanse me from my sin.
For I know my transgressions,
and my sin is always before me.
Against you, you only, have I sinned
and done what is evil in your sight;
so you are right in your verdict
and justified when you judge.
Surely I was sinful at birth
sinful from the time my mother conceived me.
Yet you desired faithfulness even in the womb;
you taught me wisdom in that secret place.
Cleanse me with hyssop, and I will be clean;
wash me, and I will be whiter than snow.
Let me hear joy and gladness;
let the bones you have crushed rejoice.
Hide your face from my sins

and blot out all my iniquity.

Create in me a pure heart, O God,

and renew a steadfast spirit within me.

Do not cast me from your presence

or take your Holy Spirit from me.

Restore to me the joy of your salvation

and grant me a willing spirit, to sustain me.

Then I will teach transgressors your ways,

so that sinners will turn back to you.

Open my lips, Lord,

and my mouth will declare your praise.

Amen.

Scripture Reference: Psalm 51:1-13, 15

Prayer for Protection

Psalm 91 is a commanding proclamation of God's promise for protection and salvation. It can be used to pray over someone else, a group of people, or ourselves. When reciting it, visualize what is written, and see God manifesting these words in your situation or in the circumstance of others. When it says, "The Lord is my refuge," mean it in your heart. Tell God, "You are my refuge!" Feel the authority given from these words, to be shielded from the "terror of night," to know He will "command his angels concerning you to guard you," and to see yourself "tread on the lion and the cobra." When all is said and done, call on Him, and know that He will answer you.

Prayer

Whoever dwells in the shelter of the Most High
will rest in the shadow of the Almighty.
I will say of the LORD,
"He is my refuge and my fortress,
my God, in whom I trust."
Surely he will save you
from the fowler's snare
and from the deadly pestilence.
He will cover you with his feathers,
and under his wings you will find refuge;
his faithfulness will be your shield and rampart.
You will not fear the terror of night,
nor the arrow that flies by day,
nor the pestilence that stalks in the darkness,
nor the plague that destroys at midday.
A thousand may fall at your side,
ten thousand at your right hand,
but it will not come near you.
You will only observe with your eyes
  and see the punishment of the wicked.
If you say, "The LORD is my refuge,"

and you make the Most High your dwelling,

no harm will overtake you,

no disaster will come near your tent.

For he will command his angels concerning you

to guard you in all your ways;

they will lift you up in their hands,

so that you will not strike your foot against a stone.

You will tread on the lion and the cobra;

you will trample the great lion and the serpent.

"Because he loves me," says the LORD,

"I will rescue him;

I will protect him, for he acknowledges my name.

He will call on me, and I will answer him;

I will be with him in trouble,

I will deliver him and honor him.

With long life I will satisfy him

and show him my salvation."

Amen.

Scripture Reference: Psalm 91

Prayer in Spiritual Warfare

The primary role of a first responder is to run toward trouble and terror to help and protect people in need. Similarly, Christians are the first responders of spiritual warfare. In times of war, famine, plague, or any other malady that affects a people, we are God's army, built for such a time. The United States of America was built on the prayers of those going to battle, those in battle, and those who prayed at home. Whether during a large-scale tragedy or the everyday difficulties of life, we have the power of God at our disposal to bring light into the darkness.

Prayer

Spirit of the Sovereign Lord, rest upon me.

Anoint me to teach good news to the poor.

Send me to bind up the broken-hearted.

Through me, proclaim freedom for the captives.

With me, release prisoners from darkness.

Make this a year of the Lord's favor.

Comfort all who mourn,

Provide for those who grieve,

Bestow on them a crown of beauty instead of ashes,

The oil of gladness instead of mourning,

And a garment of praise instead of despair.

Let all who see acknowledge

That they are a people the Lord has blessed.

Amen.

Scripture Reference: Isaiah 61:1-3, 9

Prayer for Humility

Human beings have a thirst for control. We want to control the outcomes of our actions and circumstances. It gives us comfort to believe that we can guarantee a result in an uncertain situation.

Unfortunately, we have no such power. That authority belongs to God alone. Sometimes it helps to acknowledge that, though we can undoubtedly accomplish a lot on our own, our abilities pale compared to the power and ability of the Almighty. In the end, knowing that God is in control and holding the entire world and all of us in His hand, we must remember to praise Him to avoid being overcome by pride in our own strength.

We are nothing compared to Him, and thank goodness for that, because He has far greater intellect, knowledge, wisdom, and power than we can even fathom.

Prayer

Oh, Father,

How deep are the riches of Your wisdom and knowledge!

Your judgments are unsearchable and Your paths are beyond tracing out.

Who has known the mind of the Lord?

Who has been His counselor?

What have I ever given to You,

That You should repay me?

Your ways are higher than my ways,

Your thoughts are higher than my thoughts.

If I boast about anything,

Let it be to honor You.

If I boast in a name,

Make sure it is the name above all names.

Teach me to trust in waiting on You,

And praising You in the end.

For Your glory in all things.

Amen.

Scripture Reference: Romans 11:33-35, Isaiah 55:8-9, Galatians 6:14

Prayer for a Clean Heart

The entirety of Psalm 139 is a wonderful praise and petition. In it, David acknowledged God's omniscient sovereignty. No one on earth knows us the way God does. He created us and knit us together. He has in His awareness every detail of our lives and all the thoughts we have ever had. Nothing we do or think escapes Him.

David's request of God in this Psalm was two-fold. First, he wanted to be judged fairly by the one and only Justice of all. Second, he wanted to guard against being prideful. Particularly when it feels like we are under attack, we can become defensive and blind to our own shortcomings. We are frequently susceptible to seeing the faults in others before acknowledging our own limitations. The last two verses of Psalm 139 are a short punchline to David's plea for protection against pride. It is a simple yet courageous request that can make a tremendous impact from the inside out.

Prayer

Search me, God, and know my heart;
test me and know my anxious thoughts.
See if there is any offensive way in me,
and lead me in the way everlasting.
Amen.

Scripture Reference: Psalm 139:23-24

Prayer to be Called for His Purpose

When God looks across the earth for people to carry out His purpose, we want to be counted worthy of His calling, don't we? We want our actions and pursuits to have purpose and to serve a greater good beyond ourselves. "God, I will do whatever You want me to do," we declare. Then, we go about our day doing what *we* want to do. Surrendering our will to His is the first step to living peaceful lives in the arms of our Heavenly Father.

Prayer

Heavenly Father,

Make me worthy of Your calling.

By Your power,

Fulfill every good purpose through me,

Every action prompted by faith,

So the name of our Lord Jesus

May be glorified in me,

According to Your grace.

Amen.

Scripture Reference: 2 Thessalonians 1:11-12

Prayer for Combating Evil

History has proven, time and time again, that people have an insatiable appetite for power. It is as evident today as it has ever been. The founding fathers of America recognized this human characteristic as a threat to democracy, which is why they initially structured the Articles of Confederation as simplistically as it was. That modest document eventually gave rise to the Constitution, which set up checks and balances to guard against the desire for power.

Across the world, some tyrants seek to destroy God's people by taking their freedom and turning them away from Him. The only way to overcome these earthly powers is with spiritual weapons. We must be awakened to the corruptive influence of worldly strength and combat it with the unmatched strength of the heavenly arsenal.

SCRIPTURAL PRAYERS

Prayer

Sovereign God,

Why do the nations rage and the people plot in vain?

The kings and rulers of the earth who rise up and band together against the Lord,

Lead them to fall into the very pits they dig for our destruction.

Awaken Your people!

Ignite our souls!

Give sight to eyes that are blinded from the truth!

Open ears that have been deaf to Your voice!

Write Your Word on the tongues of the muted!

Now, Lord, consider their threats,

And enable Your servants to speak Your word with great boldness.

Stretch out Your hand to heal,

And perform signs and wonders,

Through the name of Your holy servant, Jesus.

Amen.

Scripture Reference: Psalm 2:1, Psalm 7:15, Acts 4:29-30

Prayer in a Lengthy Struggle

Even after being anointed as the second king of Israel, David endured many years of struggle before he was allowed to assume the crown. He often asked God, "How long must I endure this?" After all, he was faithful. He knew God's promise. He was supposed to be king. Yet, for many years, he was running for his life, just trying to survive. There were likely moments when he thought, "It wasn't supposed to be like this."

Similarly, God repeatedly told Joshua and other leaders to "be strong and courageous." Why would God say this to the people He has called for His purpose? Because, when going through seasons of prolonged trials or deep valleys when we're unable to see the light at the end of the tunnel, we inevitably have moments of weakness and discouragement. Remember the promises of God's Word. Use those promises to provide hope in prayer, to see the light we know is there, and to give us strength to endure however long we must, until He delivers us out of the valley and into a new hope.

Prayer

How long, Lord?
How long must this wrestling go on?
Finish Your message for this season.
Call Your servant according to Your purpose,
And work these trials together for good.
Use this suffering to produce perseverance.
Through perseverance, build character.
From character, instill undying hope.
With the same Spirit that raised Jesus from the dead,
Give life to this mortal body through His Spirit.
Expose deception. Reveal truth.
Put enmity before this enemy that has risen.
Command it to flee in seven directions.
Prepare a cloak of peace in its place.
Restore strength and steadfast faith.
We take heart amid this trouble,
Let us overcome as You have overcome the world.
Do immeasurably more than all we ask or imagine,
According to Your power at work within us,
For the glory of Your power throughout all generations.
Amen.

Scripture Reference: Psalm 13:1-2, Deuteronomy 28:7, Romans 8:28, 1 Peter 5:10, Romans 5:3-4, John 16:33, Romans 8:11, Ephesians 3:20-21, Genesis 3:15

PERSONAL PRAYERS

Pray in the Spirit at all times and on every occasion. Stay alert and be persistent in your prayers for all believers everywhere.

Ephesians 6:18 NLT

There is not one way to pray. Prayers can be as short as one word or as long as needed. They can be said in an instant or over the course of hours or days. They can be full of praise or pleas. They can include any emotion—concern, gratitude, desperation, joy, frustration, or elation. What a prayer contains is up to the person who is praying. However, there are different ways to pray depending on the situation or request, and some elements will shape our focus and awareness of God's response. Let's look at some of these variables.

Salutation

We can change how we address God as we begin to pray, depending on why we are coming to Him. He is one God, but an almighty Creator with many different characteristics and unlimited power. Writers throughout the Bible address Him by many names other than "God." For instance, the name Jehovah-Rapha means "the Lord who heals," referenced for the first time in the Bible in Exodus 15:26, when God declares to the Israelites, "I am the LORD, who heals you" (NLT). If specifically asking for healing from God, we might begin our prayer by addressing Him as "Jehovah-Rapha."

After Abraham had been asked to sacrifice his son, Isaac, he was spared from following through when God stopped him and sent a young ram to sacrifice instead. Genesis 22:14 says Abraham named the place of this event "Jehovah-Jireh," meaning "The Lord will provide." Thus, a prayer in a time of need could begin by addressing God as "Jehovah-Jireh."

If we seek wisdom, we might address our prayer to our "Heavenly Father." Asking for His power, we can call out to "Almighty God." For guidance or advocacy, look to Jesus as "Lord." As we confess, He is our "Merciful Father," who delights in showing mercy (Micah 7:18). If we are in a vulnerable place, as a child looks to a parent, we might whisper, "Abba," or simply start a prayer with "Father" when we need a strong word. I (Stephanie) find myself starting prayers, "Dear God, I come to You in Jesus' name." Something is calming about beginning my prayers that way.

Whatever you decide to call God at the beginning of a prayer, take a moment to consider if it is congruent with the reason you are praying.

I want to note, don't get so caught up in the mechanics of praying that the prayer is not from the heart. God answers to any of these names and isn't going to ignore a prayer because of how we come to Him.

We are all in different stages of our relationship with God. You might have been praying since you were a child, but maybe your prayers have become stagnant and you are only going through the motions. On the other hand, you might be new to prayer or barely know what to utter. Keep coming to Him, keep showing up, and learn.

Active vs. Passive

Someone once said, "Life will pay whatever price you ask of it." Simply put, we will get what we ask for. We should approach God boldly, requesting of Him whatever we seek. The more specific we are, the clearer we will be in what we seek once we rise from our knees (or chair or wherever else we might be when praying) and become more aware of the answer that will come. Ultimately, it is His prerogative to say "Yes" or "No" or even answer in a way we never expected. Faith is trusting in His answer, even when we may not understand or like it.

As much as is appropriate, remove passive language from your prayers. What is a passive prayer? The request begins with phrases such as "Let us" or "May you." For instance, we often say, "Let us hear Your voice" or "May You grant us peace." There is absolutely nothing wrong with saying that and asking that of God. However, there are moments when we want to hear something specific or are desperate for peace. In these moments, think about *why* you need to listen to His voice or want Him to grant peace, and consider stating those requests with action words. Such as:

"God, *give me* ears to hear You when You speak, and *make it clear* to me that it is Your voice."

"Father, *strengthen us* in this time, *lift us up* on wings like eagles, and *clothe us* in the peace that passes all understanding."

Changing the words we use in our prayers can change how we see God and recognize His answers.

Just Nothing

We often include the word "just" in our prayers. It has become a common word in everyday speech and has found its way into our conversation with God. While on the surface it appears to be a humble way to make a request of God, its meaning diminishes the importance of the prayer and the reverence we have for Him. We might say, "Lord, we *just* come to You..." or "Father, we *just* thank You..." That word slips in subconsciously. We don't mean anything by it, but if we really analyze it in context, it devalues God's time and attention. It is only one word, a seemingly small nuance, but one that can completely alter our perspective when communing with God. If we use it to be polite in our beseeching, it might reveal an underlying hesitation inside of us and a disrespect to Almighty God in essentially saying, "I'm *just* asking for this little thing; won't You grant it?"

Why would we approach the Creator of the universe, the heavens, and the earth and ask for a tiny little thing? He wants to give us much, so why not ask for much? He "gives generously to all without finding fault" (James 1:5). Boldly and courageously, let us set our prayers before God, knowing He can do abundantly more than we could ever ask or imagine.

Closing

As there are many ways to address God at the beginning of a prayer, there are also various ways and reasons by which we can conclude a prayer. The question is, why should He grant us this request?

Throughout the writings of the prophets in the Old Testament, God repeatedly described what was going to happen and what He was going to do, concluding many declarations with, "Then they will know that I am the Lord." There is always a greater reason why God does what He does. We should consider the more significant reason why we want God to answer our prayers by having our eyes on His Kingdom and an eternal view.

Whatever we say or ask for in our prayers, we can always conclude with one of the following:

"In Jesus' name."

"In the name of the Father, Son, and Holy Spirit."

"For Your honor and glory."

"So they will know that You are the Lord."

"For the benefit and expansion of Your Kingdom."

"For Your name to be lifted and praised."

"For the glory of Jesus, in whose name we pray and believe together."

However you choose to address God and whatever you want to say or request, take a moment to prepare before you begin. It could be a few seconds or a minute to consider what you are going to pray about before approaching the almighty, all-knowing, ever-present Creator of all things. Taking time to center yourself will help you become more present, hear better, and find the peace or praise you seek when you pray.

I (Stephanie) like to sit in the stillness of silence. Take pause. Stare out the window. Not rush my conversation or encounter with God. This is a great way to start the day. Learn to step away from the hurry of life and give God the attention He deserves.

At first, sitting still might be hard. We live in a culture that is not used to sitting still, especially with no phone in our hands. But the more we do this, the easier it will become. Our souls will crave the time with our Heavenly Father. As Psalm 46:10 reminds us, "He says, 'Be still, and know that I am God.'"

Prayer Moment (Mike)

When my mother was nearing the end of her battle against cancer, I made one brief but substantial request of God more than any other: "Father, send her angels." Many instances are written in the scriptures of angels visiting human beings, often in dreams and sometimes in physical form. I didn't know exactly what that would look like or what it would mean if God were to answer my prayer, but I believed that He could do it. So I asked directly for Him to send her angels to provide whatever she needed, when she needed it.

I was overwhelmingly grateful to witness Him repeatedly answer that prayer through people who showed up at the right time. Whether through personal visits, phone calls, or aid and support, time and time again God sent angels to provide for my mother, often during desperate and difficult situations. I had asked Him to send angels, and it was too obvious not to notice that He sent people in astounding ways.

Ask, and you shall receive. Our responsibility is to ask and then receive however God chooses to respond. Trust Him. He knows what we need much better than we do and is faithful.

Prayer for Purpose and Direction

"What is my purpose, Lord? What do You want me to do? Tell me, and I will do it. I need to know."

We all have likely said this or something similar. It is not for a lack of guidance on God's part that we fail to follow Him. Unfortunately, fear, apathy, and selfishness often keep us from following what God calls us to do. It is easy to feel that we are less than other people and that we haven't been given gifts at the same level that others seem to possess. However, God does not create something for nothing. If we take an honest assessment of our lives, we will see that He has given us abilities and has been with us in good times and bad. We may not know exactly why or to what end, but we can be confident that He has given us life to be used for good.

Prayer

Heavenly Father,
You created me from nothing,
Called me for this moment in time,
Led me through the valley,
To the mountain too,
Down and back again.
You equipped me with knowledge,
Placed conviction in my heart.
I don't know why.
I don't know how.
I don't know for whom.
Whatever Your purpose is,
Here I am.
Speak, and I will listen.
Reveal yourself, and I will see.
Order me, and I will go.
I lay down every selfish desire,
Every extraneous excuse,
Every irrational fear.
My life is Yours to use,
To do exceedingly,

Abundantly more,

Then I could ask or imagine.

Amen.

Scripture Reference: Psalm 23:4, Isaiah 6:8, 1 Samuel 3:10, Ephesians 3:20

Prayer to Search for Meaning

King Solomon is known to have had greater wisdom than anyone who has walked the earth. He used it to gain material and experiential wealth. Yet, he viewed everything he had gained and accomplished as meaningless. Our lives, or at least portions of them, can feel that way.

"Why bother?" is a battle cry we bellow when frustrated, defeated, and pondering the importance of our toil. However, why would God have bothered to create us, especially for the time He did, for no reason? There is a great purpose for our lives. Whether or not it is visible to us, God is at work.

We (Mike and Stephanie) never had a plan to write books. But both of us felt God laying callings on our hearts, and we put in the time and effort to write out and share the messages God has given us. We know that God is at work in the lives of those who read the words we've written. Writing books often is not fun—the process is long and laborious—but this is one purpose God has for our lives, and we are trusting Him and walking in faith with each book we publish.

Think back to your younger years. What got you excited? What brings you joy now? Maybe it's gardening, writing, singing, running, or numbers. Whatever your muse, ask yourself, "Am I doing what God created me to do? Or am I wasting time on social media, binging Netflix, or continuing at a job that is not using the strengths and talents God gave me?"

PERSONAL PRAYERS

If you are questioning whether you are living out your purpose, use this prayer (or one of your own) to allow God to lead you in discovering how you are to be spending time here on earth.

Prayer

Heavenly Father,

My eyes search for significance,

My heart longs for purpose,

My hands toil through time.

Why does everything under the sun seem meaningless

Until You reveal its great worth?

For this moment in time,

Reveal to me the purpose You have for my life.

Use my efforts for everlasting mission.

Turn my impatience into enduring light.

Show me where I am wasting time.

Reveal through me Your eternal mysteries.

Take all that I am,

And all that I do,

And use me in this time, in this place, with Your people,

In what is meaningful to You.

Amen.

Scripture Reference: Ecclesiastes 1:2, Esther 4:14

Prayer for Perspective

Constant distractions surround us, and we cling so tightly to what we see in front of us. We have habitual thoughts, often contrary to what we believe and value, that cause confusion. Impulsive emotions deceive us. If we aren't careful, our eyes will determine our reality, but what we physically see is not the only true reality. We forget that God is invisibly at work, impacting what is visible.

We must remind ourselves that God is everywhere, working all the time. We need to slow down, unclog our ears, and open our eyes to focus on His invisible power amid the chaos and confusion. That perspective will bring peace to our hearts and in situations throughout our daily lives.

Prayer

Speak, Lord, Your servant is listening.
My ears distort. My eyes deceive. My mind misleads.
Take my every thought captive.
Slow me down.
Untangle the webs of confusion within.
Unblur my vision to see You everywhere
And to recognize Your ever-working hand
In the messiness of each moment.
Be more real than the reality I perceive.
Show me Your presence, and allow me to see You.
Teach me to delight in the richness of Your mercy and grace.
Amen.

Scripture Reference: 1 Samuel 3:10, 2 Corinthians 10:5, Ephesians 2:4-5

Prayer for Seeking God

In the Psalms, David often pleaded with God during difficult times. He cried out for help and protection. He called to God in desperation when it seemed God was not there, even though David knew God was always with him.

God is open to hearing our petitions and complaints. It is okay to admit that we can't see Him, that it seems as if He is not involved in our daily lives or with us in our pain. Even John the Baptist had a moment of doubt, in Matthew 11:3, asking Jesus, "'Are you the one who is to come, or should we expect someone else?'"

If it seems like God is not involved in our daily life, we must do some soul searching and ask ourselves, "Are *we* involving *God* in our daily life?" If not, we must evaluate our priorities and put God at the top.

God promises that if we seek Him with all our heart, we will find Him (Jeremiah 29:13). If we do our part in the relationship and seek Him, we will find Him always right next to us.

Prayer

Heavenly Father,

I am calling on You, coming to You, praying to You.

Open my heart to listen to You.

Not only to hear, but also to be still and listen.

I will seek You with all my heart,

Look for You as for silver,

Search as for a hidden treasure.

Show me where You are.

Let me find You in everything I do,

To reveal You to a broken and lost world

In desperate need to be in Your presence.

Amen.

Scripture Reference: Psalm 31:1, Psalm 5:1-2, Psalm 86:6, Psalm 81:13-14, Jeremiah 29:12-13, Proverbs 2:4

Prayer for Spiritual Sight

Regardless of what is happening to and around us, our reality depends on what we focus on. Do we choose to see life or death? Blessings or curses? The goodness of God or the darkness of evil? If we dwell only on what our eyes can see, that will be our only reality. Our physical eyes often see darkness, pain, suffering, and trials. However, that is not the constant truth. Everything in the world that we see with our eyes changes; it does not remain but all withers away.

Our eyes will deceive us if we are not intentional in our focus. We will end up "judging a book by its cover," without knowing what is on the inside. What is the immediate thought and action you take when you see a homeless person on the side of the road? Do you think, "Get a job!" and turn your head? Or do you think, "I wonder what hardships this person has gone through in life to lead them to begging on the side of the road"? Do you make eye contact, giving a smile and a little wave? On numerous occasions when I (Stephanie) have smiled and waved at someone on the sidewalk or street corner, they've smiled back and waved. And then I wonder, is it money they need or the love of Jesus Christ?

Only God is absolute and constant truth. He is the only unchangeable, unmovable certainty. Hebrews 13:8 says, "Jesus Christ is the same yesterday, today, and forever" (NLT). Seeking Him in all situations is the only way to lead us to the truth around us; finding Him will allow us to see and know the truth of everything.

Prayer

Almighty God,
Creator of all things,
Teach me to seek You with all my heart,
So that I will find You where You are,
And know truth.
Put Your lens over my eyes
To see the world as You see it,
To peer into the hearts of people,
To understand Your view of them.
When I am lost, show me the way.
Where there is confusion, bring clarity.
When there is discord, build harmony.
For freedom, set me free.
Lead me to repentance, renewal, and rejoicing.
I will praise you in the calm
And in the storm.
For You are with me through it all.
Amen.

Scripture Reference: Jeremiah 29:13, 1 Samuel 16:7, 1 Corinthians 14:33, Galatians 5:1, Psalm 34:1

Prayer for Belief in the Unseen

God is all around us. He is involved in everything we do; from the moment we wake in the morning until we lay our heads to sleep at night. Even then, He is still at work while we rest. As Psalm 121:4 says, God "will neither slumber nor sleep."

It is easy to pray in the morning, only to forget His presence as we go about our day. Our physical senses tend to challenge our capacity to believe in the spiritual. We often see the world around us out of fear, selfishness, or lack of faith and perceive, presume, or believe a false reality. Let go of those emotions, and know that our eyes only observe a small part of the story.

We must not forget that God operates in the physical *and* spiritual realms, with the spiritual influencing our lives in much more profound and powerful ways than the physical.

Get in the habit of looking for and seeking God's goodness throughout the day. The more we look, the more we will see Him. The more we talk with Him, the more we recognize His voice.

Prayer

Lord, my eyes deceive me.

Forgive me for taking my focus off You

And for believing more in what I see

Than in what You are doing in the midst of everything.

I want to return to believing

More in what my eyes cannot see

Than in what the world looks like around me.

I do believe,

Help my unbelief.

Amen.

Scripture Reference: 2 Corinthians 4:18, Mark 9:24

Prayer for Clarity

In our daily lives and in the world around us, the truth about anything is difficult to recognize. What we see, feel, or experience is often confusing and unclear. We have too many inputs and pundits with their own agendas filling our social media and news feeds. God is the only source of truth we can trust. When bewildered or frustrated by the inability to know what is true and false, cry out to Him for understanding. If we doubt or have an unsettling feeling in our spirit about what we see and hear, we must open our Bible and ask, "Does this message I am receiving align with what the Word of God says?" God's Word is the only truth we can stand on and trust.

Prayer

Almighty God,

Let the truth arise!

Shout it from the rooftops!

Let it be heard.

Reveal the truth of my own heart.

Speak it to my ears,

Show it to my eyes,

Remove any blinders,

Expose any lies,

Put it on my tongue.

Set me free,

With the One and Only truth there is!

Amen.

Scripture Reference: Matthew 10:27, John 8:32, Psalm 23-24, Acts 9:18

Prayer for Trust and Obedience

How much do we miss because we hesitate to do something God asks of us? We may hear a soft voice or a loud conviction that grips our hearts tightly, but we fail to act.

New parents are taught the concept of "first-time obedience" with their children. It is a form of discipline to train them to obey commands the first time they are given. That is what God wants of us. He has a plan, He knows best, and it is much better for us if we do what He says, the first time. Abraham did not balk when God asked him to go. When God told Mary she would have a child, she replied, "I am the Lord's servant; may your word to me be fulfilled." Look what miracles were ahead, simply because they said "Yes" and without hesitation willingly took the action God asked of them.

When I (Stephanie) went on my giving journey, giving a gift every day for 522 days, I often prayed, "God, show me who I'm supposed to give to today." And without fail, He would answer. However, I quickly learned that giving takes courage to engage with strangers and offer them help. Every time I got the nudge to approach a stranger, I had to trust God had a reason for putting me in this person's path and then obey Him by acting. Over and over again, God showed me that when we trust and obey Him, He will use us in incredible ways to make a difference to those around us, showing others the love of Jesus.

Prayer

Lord,
Whatever You ask of me today,
Give me the will to comply.
Forgive me for arguing with You at times,
Being selfish or afraid,
Not yielding to Your requests or plan.
I trust in You alone.
Forgive me that my actions have not shown that trust.
Mold me into one who will be as Abraham and Mary,
Instantly, obediently taking action,
Without argument,
Without negotiating,
Without fear,
Without doubt,
Without hesitating.
My heart is in Your hands
For Your will to be done,
With me,
Through me,
On earth as it is in heaven.
Amen.
Scripture Reference: Genesis 26:4-5, Luke 1:38, Matthew 6:10

Prayer for Repentance

Repentance is an act of turning away from sin (such as pride, lust, greed, envy, gluttony, wrath, and sloth) or a godless way of life and returning to a more fervent obedience to the Lord. We must deny our temptation to engage in behaviors that keep us from God and replace them with disciplined obedience to His instruction.

To be obedient, we must first know what He wants from us. He is always instructing, rebuking, and guiding us. Even when the learning process might be uncomfortable, asking Him to teach us opens us to a greater knowledge of His truth in our lives. With that knowledge, we can change our actions. Then God will change our hearts, removing the desire for unwanted behavior.

Often, we pray for God to remove the desire first, so that by removing the desire, our negative actions will change. However, if we change our actions and ask God to alter our heart simultaneously, the change will become transformational.

Prayer

Lord,

Teach me to deny myself more often.

Teach me to be stronger against the world.

Teach me to see my sin.

Teach me to want only You and no more of my sin.

Teach me to find satisfaction in You.

Teach me to understand the joy of the Lord.

Teach me to rest in obedience to the truth.

Teach me to love unselfishly.

Teach me to let go undeniably.

Show me where to seek Your righteousness.

Change my heart as I change my actions.

Amen.

Scripture Reference: Psalm 86:11, Matthew 4:17, Romans 6:23

Prayer for Freedom from Worry

We tend to trust God with our eternity but worry about the daily aspects of life. If we are willing to put our salvation in His hands, why would we not do the same with our interactions and circumstances day after day? Jesus instructed us not to worry, which suggests that worrying is a sin. How could that be? Because worry demonstrates a lack of faith and trust in the Almighty.

Declaring our beliefs and intentions to God will help align our faith in the big and small things. Just as writing down our goals and plans creates positive momentum toward them, speaking our beliefs out loud and declaring them to God creates unseen power as we walk through each day confidently, as a warrior and not a worrier.

Prayer

Heavenly Father,

I have been fearful in quiet places,

Too afraid of daily circumstances,

Too worried about trivial consequences.

What can man do to me?

If You are for me, who can be against me?

I am convinced that nothing in this life,

No opposition or temptation,

Can separate me from your love.

Convict my heart with bold faith,

In the still, small moments of each day!

In praise and honor for Your love and goodness,

Amen.

Scripture Reference: Psalm 118:6, Romans 8:31-39

Prayer for Embracing Discomfort

We typically try to avoid undue pressure, discomfort, and pain, don't we? After all, uncomfortable situations aren't tempting predicaments to be in. Unfortunately, those are the methods by which God often works. To build muscle, we must be willing to push against weight that is beyond comfortable. To grow, we must explore and expand beyond where we feel most secure. A powerful way to begin embracing the challenges and trials that will help us grow is to simply say, "I'm sorry," for running from them.

Prayer

Father, forgive me for avoiding pressure,

For complaining about obstacles,

For running from the storms,

For seeking comfort.

Take this rock You created,

Use the pressure to make me stronger,

To expand my faith,

To bring me closer to You,

To grow in my empathy,

To become more compassionate.

Form a diamond that shines your brilliant light.

In Jesus' name I pray,

Amen.

Scripture Reference: James 1:2-4, Matthew 4:1-11, Luke 4:1-13

Prayer to Face the Storm

Many of us work hard to evade difficult paths and uncomfortable situations. The irony of this approach is that it leads farther into the pit of struggle, exacerbating the very challenges and obstacles that we try so hard to dodge. Eventually, the only way to escape the difficulty is to go through it.

If, when we meet God, He asks how we enjoyed the human experience He allowed us to live, we don't want our answer to be, "Well, I tried to avoid most of it." To experience the fullness of this life for which we have been created, we must go through the ups and downs, pains and pleasures, trials and triumphs. A storm makes us appreciate a sunny day with blue skies. Through our suffering, He prepares us for the goodness He has in store for us. If we try to temper the terrain or control the outcomes too much, we will miss the grand adventure, the lessons, and the character-building God has planned for us along the way.

Prayer

Abba,

Forgive me for trusting myself
To create what I think You want from me.

Forgive me for trying to control the results of my actions.

Forgive me for practicing avoidance,
For seeking a way around,
When the only way is through.

I surrender all outcomes to Your mighty hand.

Through me, craft what You desire.

Lead me...

To experience the pains of the world
And the joy of overcoming.

To know the disappointment of my limitations
And the gratitude for Your almighty power.

To sense the unknowing anticipation of what is to come
And the exultation of deliverance.

To feel the strain of hard work
And the beauty of Your workmanship.

I want to experience the loss of control in my own life
And the glory of being resurrected in Yours.

Take my life, and make it Your own.

Amen.

PERSONAL PRAYERS

Scripture Reference: Proverbs 16:18, Ephesians 2:10, Matthew 10:39

Prayer to Address Pride

We all feel inadequate, afraid that people will find out we are not nearly as knowledgeable as they might think, or as good as they hope we are. While that emotion may seem like insecurity, it is rooted in pride. How? Because we have a desire to present ourselves as infallible, even when it is not an accurate representation of who we are.

Proverbs 16:18 warns that "Pride goes before destruction." Call pride out and speak to it. Then embrace your imperfections. You were perfectly created with those deficiencies to be a living example of the perfect power of God. Don't hide that power. Tell pride and fear to go, and ask God to use His strength through you. Remember, when we are weak, He is strong.

Prayer

Father, I have been proud.

Too proud to admit what I lack.

Too proud to show my weaknesses.

Too afraid to admit the truth.

Reveal any pride I am too blind to see.

But what I lack, You fulfill.

Allow my weaknesses to make Your power known.

Remind me that my weakness is Your strength.

The meek have an inheritance.

We are descendants of the King.

Heirs of His majesty.

Father, use me to be a living boast of Your greatness!

Amen.

Scripture Reference: 2 Corinthians 12:9, Romans 8:17
Matthew 5:5, 1 Corinthians 1:31

Prayer to Know How God Sees Me

We spend a lot of mental energy wondering what other people think of us. At the same time, we beat ourselves up for our shortcomings and mistakes. God is the only one who knows who we were created to be. We take so much time worrying about other people's perceptions and so little time asking God His opinion. Yet, His is the only opinion that matters.

Usually, we are wrong in what we believe people think about us. We see the worst in ourselves and forget we are created in the image of God.

God is not disappointed in what He created. He might be discouraged by our choices, but the Creator does not say to His creation, "You are a terrible mistake." What comfort and love there is in asking Him to tell us about the person He created in us. We can ask Him to describe what He created in us, then be quiet and listen. We will know when we hear from Him. His response may not come in the moment, but if we pray continuously and keep asking and seeking the answer, He will reveal it.

Prayer

Heavenly Father,

My heart is soft.

My ears are open.

Tell me, Lord, what You think of me.

I see myself in many ways,

And the world views me through its lens,

But You created me.

How do You see me?

Who am I in Your eyes?

Tell me the truth.

Tell me about me.

I am listening to Your voice alone.

Amen.

Scripture Reference: Genesis 1:27, Colossians 3:10, Psalm 139:17-18

Prayer for Gratitude in Adversity

We tend to forget the pathway to growth is through adversity. We try to avoid pain and discomfort as much as possible. However, building muscle requires using that muscle past the point of comfort, when it becomes difficult and often painful. We all face challenges in life. We all go through seasons that we wish we didn't have to experience. The pain and difficulty are wasted if we fail to recognize and learn from the lessons and forego the growth those seasons offer.

One way to get over the hurt of the past or the frustration of the moment is to be authentically grateful for the challenges. Those times have a purpose in improving us if we remain faithful in loving God and embracing His purpose for our lives.

Prayer

Heavenly Father,

Thank you for the struggles of life.

Thank you for the adversity and pain.

Thank you for pruning me.

Thank you for not giving me everything I want,

Even when I tell You I want it.

Thank you for making me think deeper.

Thank you for giving me strength.

Thank you for leading me to become better.

May Your Kingdom come and Your will be done,

Through me, around me, and inside me,

As it is in heaven.

Amen.

Scripture Reference: 2 Corinthians 4:17, John 15:2, Matthew 6:9-13

Prayer of Thankfulness

If we have regular prayer time, we will likely have experiences of entering prayer and realizing that we don't have anything to ask for at that moment. Of course, there is always something we could ask or someone we can lift up, but sometimes a declaration of gratitude is enough.

Gratitude reminds us how thankful we are, and should be, for all that God has done and continues to do for us.

Prayer

Thank you, Lord.

Thank you for taking the sting of death.

Thank you for loosing the grip of fear.

Thank you for eternal hope.

Thank you for offering the power of Your Spirit.

Thank you for giving authority through prayer.

Thank you for Your love and grace.

Thank you for Your patience.

Thank you for taking brokenness,

And resurrecting it into a full life.

Thank you for entering the tomb,

And then leaving it empty,

To come get me.

Amen.

Scripture Reference: 1 Corinthians 15:55

SHORT PRAYERS

"When you pray, don't babble on and on as the Gentiles do. They think their prayers are answered merely by repeating their words again and again."

Matthew 6:7 NLT

Prayers can be as simple as one powerful word or a brief sentence. There is a scene in the movie *Ever After* in which Drew Barrymore's character, a poor maid, is about to approach a prince to ask for a favor. This type of interaction was unheard of then; a lowly maid wouldn't even dare speak to someone in the royal family, much less make a request. Just before walking up to the prince, she stopped briefly and, with conviction, whispered, "Lord, give me strength." What a prayer! Notice, she didn't ask for favor or for the interaction to be easy. Rather, she asked for the strength to do it.

So often we ask God to deliver us from an uncomfortable moment or situation so we can avoid having to endure it. We ask God to keep us from the valleys or to lead us around or over them. Even Jesus made this request in the Garden of Gethsemane, saying, "'Father, if you are willing, take this cup from me; yet not my will, but yours be done'" (Luke 22:42). Though He asked God to take Him out of the suffering, He was willing to go through it if that was what God wanted. Then Luke 22:43 tells us, "An angel from heaven appeared to him and strengthened him."

Instead of praying only to be delivered *from* a difficult or painful moment, ask God to give you what you'll need to go *through* it or what He wants you to learn from the trial. We may be praying against God's will when we pray to avoid something. The difficulties we face are often for our benefit, to grow or fulfill a greater purpose. Remember, "In all things God works for the good of those who love Him, who have been called according to his purpose" (Romans 8:28). God leads us *through* the valleys in life, not just *to* the valleys. Whether we need strength, faith, endurance, wisdom, knowledge, or anything else, He will provide us with whatever we need to accomplish His perfect will in our lives.

Prayer Moment (Stephanie)

I have stepped onto hundreds of stages and spoken to thousands of people. In the early years of my speaking career, when I was introduced, I would walk up on stage and then start my talk.

Years back, as I sat on the front pew of a church, waiting for the pastor to call my name, I felt the Holy Spirit asking me to bow my head in prayer.

I must admit, I hesitated a bit, as I was more concerned about what the congregation behind me would think than being obedient to the calling of the Holy Spirit.

The urge was so strong, I bowed my head and prayed, "Lord, give me the words to speak, and open the hearts and minds of the people here. Calm my nerves. Thank you for this message. Amen."

When the pastor called my name, I rose and confidently walked up to the pulpit, opened my Bible, took a deep breath, and shared my message.

I can't describe the difference I felt, but it made such an impact that now I always bow my head to pray before I take the stage. I prayed before I walked out on the TEDx stage and again before I stood center court in a gymnasium full of high schoolers. My prayers are not limited to my speaking in a church. I hope my action, of bowing my head and closing my eyes, in public, is a way to boldly communicate my faith and the power of prayer to those around me.

No matter where you are and what you are doing, take God along for the ride. He'll bring you a calming peace like you have never experienced before.

Prayer for Direction and Guidance

King Solomon wrote in Proverbs 16:9, "A man's heart plans his way, but the Lord directs his steps" (NKJV). When we ask God for guidance, it can seem easier to sit and wait for Him to provide a prompt or sign, but rarely, if ever, does that produce a result. Solomon instructs us to make our plans and trust God to guide us as we begin taking action.

How do we do that?

One way is to ask Him to reveal open and closed doors and make it crystal clear which are open and which are closed.

For example, if we ask God to close doors that He doesn't want us to walk through, we can ask Him to slam them shut. We want a loud noise and a forceful smash! Even if that door were in a direction we wanted to take—like a job we thought would provide more money, opportunity, or growth—if He clearly closes the door, let's praise Him. We want to stay clear of paths He does not want us to go down.

If a door closes, it might be closed forever. We don't want to pry it open or barrel it down because we are too impatient to wait for an opening. God might have a better opportunity we aren't aware of, and we never know what He may be protecting us from. Sometimes the answer is "not now," perhaps as a test to ensure we trust Him. We must be patient until we arrive at the doors He wants us to enter.

It's important to note that when we ask God for directions, we must give up control of the outcome. He may open the door to something scary that we would normally avoid. We do not pray to manifest an open or closed door that fits our wishes, but rather we pray to submit to the direction God wants us to follow.

How will we know which direction to go or not go? First, we must have a relationship with God to know His voice and recognize the nudging of the Holy Spirit. Second, we might experience an unexpected peace. Maybe we wanted to go one way, but when the door was closed or another way presented itself, a calming sense washed over us and we knew that was an answer from God.

We can't see where we are going, but He can.

Life will get easier if we pray before making decisions and then completely yield all control to God to lead us down the right path.

Prayer

Father,

Open doors that You want me to walk through,

And close doors that don't fit Your plan.

Make it clear to me,

For You are not a God of confusion,

But a God of clarity and peace.

Order my steps to align with Your will.

Amen.

Scripture Reference: Colossians 4:3, 1 Corinthians 14:33

Prayer for Help in Any Situation

At various times in our lives, we all feel inadequate, that we don't know enough, we don't belong, we aren't equipped or we don't have enough ability. Here's the good news... we aren't adequate! That doesn't mean our worth is diminished. It means we do not have to be perfect—because we never will be.

When we find ourselves in these situations, we can call on an omniscient God to accomplish what we cannot do by our own power, because with God, nothing is impossible. This doesn't mean that we shouldn't prepare as best we can. It means that when we've prepared but still feel insufficient for the task at hand, we can relinquish any reliance on our ability and knowledge, trusting that God can and will work through us. Therefore, when going into a work meeting, stepping into a leadership situation, trying to solve a difficult problem, or having a difficult conversation with a friend or family member—and feeling as if we do not have enough to fulfill that role—we can take comfort in knowing that God can raise our ability. We, in ourselves, will never be enough, but God can do more than enough through us.

Prayer

Heavenly Father,

Without You I am inadequate,

But with You, all things are possible.

Transform me into something more than I can be on my own.

Not by might,

Nor by power,

But by Your Spirit.

Amen.

Scripture Reference: Matthew 19:26, Zechariah 4:6

Prayer for The Lord's Blessing

After God led the Israelites out of hundreds of years of Egyptian slavery, He commissioned them to follow Him. In return, He would deliver them into the promised land, a land flowing with milk and honey. While sharing guidelines for the Israelites to live by, God instructed Moses and Aaron on how they should bless the people. Then God said, "'So they will put my name on the Israelites, and I will bless them'" (Numbers 6:27).

What better way to seek the blessings of the Almighty than by His own counsel? This is a beautiful prayer that can be said over anyone who is sick, going through a trying time, setting out to accomplish a worthy goal, or any life circumstance at any time. We pray that God will be with them as they walk out His calling and commission.

Prayer

The LORD bless you and keep you;

the LORD make his face shine on you and be gracious to you;

the LORD turn his face toward you

and give you peace.

Amen.

Scripture Reference: Numbers 6:24-26

Prayer to Prepare for the Lord

In today's world, we have pundits, commentators, reporters, and analysts whose job it is to talk up future stars, be they athletes, politicians, business leaders, or anyone else who appears to be a prodigy. John the Baptist was called to that role in his day, to talk up Jesus and prepare people for His future ministry.

Similarly, as believers, we know that Jesus is coming back to the earth, and it is our calling to prepare others for that time, for we know that His return will come when people do not expect it. The Great Commission that Jesus gave to His disciples (and to us) is for that very purpose.

What is the Great Commission? We learn about it in Matthew 28:18-20. "Jesus came and told his disciples, 'I have been given all authority in heaven and on earth. Therefore, go and make disciples of all the nations, baptizing them in the name of the Father and the Son and the Holy Spirit. Teach these new disciples to obey all the commands I have given you. And be sure of this: I am with you always, even to the end of the age'" (NLT).

Where does the preparation for the Lord's return begin? In the home. An angel visited John the Baptist's father, Zechariah, to inform him about his son's purpose—first, to turn the attention of fathers to their children; and second, to make disciples, helping those who don't know Jesus to change their lives by gaining wisdom that comes from the only righteous One. That assignment is still active and the most impactful agent of positive change in the world.

Prayer

In the spirit and power of Elijah,
Turn the hearts of the fathers to their children
And the disobedient to the wisdom of the righteous—
To make ready a people prepared for the Lord.
Amen.

Scripture Reference: Luke 1:17, Matthew 28:16-20

Prayer for Successful Outcomes

Research shows that our words have ten times more power than our thoughts. On a grander scale, we know that one hundred percent of what God says He will do, He will do. Nothing He speaks into existence will fail to return to Him unfulfilled. When we declare an ambition and set out to do it, we can call on God to use those words to set in motion an outcome that accomplishes His purpose.

Similarly, we can call on God to fulfill His word and His promise. We are earnestly pleading, "God, You said this… Let Your words not remain empty, but accomplish the purpose for which You spoke them."

Prayer

Father,

The word that goes out from my mouth:

Let it not return to me empty,

But accomplish what You desire,

And achieve the purpose for which it is sent.

Amen.

Scripture Reference: Isaiah 55:11

Prayer for Travel Guidance

Billions of people worldwide travel to familiar places every single day—to work, shop, visit relatives or vacation spots, and many other typical locations. Why is it that when we travel to a new location or a greater distance than usual, or take a trip with a specific purpose or mission in mind, we're more likely to ask for prayers for "safe travel"?

Are we truly seeking safety along the way, or is there something deeper at the heart of that request?

We could be apprehensive about the travel, such as having a fear of flying, or have trepidation about the destination. Scripture tells us that God has legions of angels at His disposal, and He can send them ahead of us to lead and clear pathways for us. They can also prepare for us, such as preparing people for our arrival and preparing the destination to receive us for the intended purpose of the trip. (See Exodus 23-20.) In this prayer, we are releasing control over the exact route and method of travel to be taken and the outcome when we arrive. It is a simple prayer for supernatural guidance. Ultimately, we want to arrive at the place *God* has prepared for us, rather than the place at which *we* hope to arrive; and we want it all to be prepared to accomplish His purpose, not our own.

Prayer

Father,
Send Your angels ahead of me,
To guard me along the way,
And to bring me to the place You have prepared.
Amen.

Scripture Reference: Exodus 23:20

Prayer in Restless Desire

Seeing the pain and suffering all around us doesn't take much effort. Understanding how we can help is often more difficult. How can we make a positive difference when there is so much anguish and many people are hurting?

Sometimes we are so overwhelmed by the need that instead of taking action we are paralyzed and do nothing. The desire to help, to do something, to do anything, can stay bottled up inside of us, creating a whirlwind of emotion. We cry to God, "Here I am, use me!" We are willing to go, but don't know where to start. Wherever and whenever, we can ask God to lead us into the fray, and He will.

Prayer

Father,

My feet are restless.

My heart is eager.

I want to go, to help, to be useful.

By your Spirit, make a way,

Deliver healing, and create answers

To our light and momentary troubles.

Let us know that you are here,

And you are God.

Amen.

Scripture Reference: Isaiah 43:16, 2 Corinthians 4:17

INTENTIONAL PRAYERS

See that no one pays back evil for evil, but always try to do good to each other and to all people. Always be joyful. Never stop praying. Be thankful in all circumstances, for this is God's will for you who belong to Christ Jesus.

1 Thessalonians 5:15-18 NLT

Sometimes we pray generally, as with the Lord's Prayer, and sometimes we pray for a need in the moment. Other times, we make intentional requests for ourselves, someone else, or a certain situation and circumstance. These prayers are aimed at a mark. They aren't general or overarching. With these, we wouldn't be praying for children overall; we would be praying for a specific thing for the children or a specific situation for one child. There is a target at which we are aiming, like shooting an arrow at a bullseye. We are going on the offensive against an attack on whatever and whomever we are praying about.

There is an authority in bringing to light the challenges we face, calling them out, speaking firmly against them, and speaking confidently for the alternative. Like taking the first step in overcoming an addiction, we admit we have a problem.

When we face a problem or difficult circumstance, our first reaction is often denial. As a result, our prayers for that problem might be tempered. By denying that the problem is anything of significance, we pray as if it's not a big deal, until we reach the point of admitting it is a big deal. That is when we become more aggressive in our prayers.

Often, these are situations we have little or no control over, like diagnosing a terminal illness. Our ability to control the desired outcome is limited, at best. We are sure of one thing—without God's intervention and power, a resolution may not occur. That is the beauty of prayer. Even when we seemingly have no control—as with disease, addiction, or oppression—we have authority over whatever threatens us because we have the power of Jesus' name. In His will, we conquer anything in this world for His purposes.

Prayer Moment (Mike)

Something wasn't right. There was discord in our family—a lack of peace in our house. I was the only one awake downstairs. Everyone else was upstairs in bed. I could feel a heaviness as I sat there. I looked around, perplexed at how we had gotten to this place of unrest. It was as if the walls were closing in.

Then it hit me. Maybe they were closing in, not literally, but spiritually, because of unseen forces pushing against them for years from the outside.

One by one, I thought about the neighbors on each side of our house, some now gone and some still there. House by house, I weighed who and what has been around us. It was revealing. In the decade and a half we lived there, we were surrounded by addiction, divorce, brokenness, hatred, fear, and illness. Not once had I prayed that those influences remain distant from our family. Perhaps, after all those years, whatever spirits had been working against our neighbors had been pressing against our home too and were starting to find their way in. I didn't know how much validity there was to that theory, but I wouldn't let another day go by without doing something about it.

On that early morning, while my family was still asleep, I walked around the bottom floor of our home, stopped at each window, held out my hands, and prayed against any evil spirits—against discord, addictions, hate, fear, and disease. I spoke to those demonic spirits to let them know they were not welcome in our house. I invited the Holy

Spirit, and *only* the Holy Spirit, into our home. I called on the authority of Jesus of Nazareth as the leader of our family to push back any dark and unholy influences that might have been having their way with us. Then I stood at the bottom of the steps that led to the top level of the house, looked up to where the rest of my family was sleeping, and declared, with the words Jesus spoke to His disciples when He appeared to them in the upper room, "Peace be with you." I concluded this prayer time by repeating that promise, again and again, "Peace be with you, peace be with you."

A few hours later, a brand-new day began, a remarkable contrast to the previous day. The discord had diminished. Hearts opened. Peace rested on us all. The feeling is difficult to describe, but it was such a stark difference from one day to the next that it was impossible to deny. Between the time we went to sleep and when we awoke, nothing had happened that would have changed everything—except prayer.

Like any family, we still have difficulties and challenges. We still have disagreements and concerns. But also, we can still see God answering those prayers and guiding us through it all.

The prayer I prayed that morning is one I encourage you to pray in your home as well.

Prayer for Protecting Your Home

When it feels that we or our family are being attacked and one thing after another keeps happening against us, it can seem that the difficulties will never end. Thankfully, we can start taking dominion over these powers because we can request authority above it all. In Mark 9:29, after Jesus had driven a demon out of a boy, He informed His disciples, "This kind can come out only by prayer." In these situations, we can claim the power that we call upon, speak directly to any ungodly influences on the attack, and drive them out in His name.

Prayer

Jehovah,

I call on Your authority over all things.

Holy Spirit,

I invite You into our midst,

I welcome You into our lives.

Rid us of every dark oppression.

Drive out any unholy spirits from our presence.

Whatever is causing illness, you are not welcome among us.

Spirit of addiction, you are not wanted, flee!

Spirit of fear, you have no power over us, flee!

Spirit of hate, you have no place here, flee!

Spirit of confusion, your influence will not affect us.

From whatever direction you come,

You turn and flee in seven!

As for this house,

We serve the Lord.

By His almighty power

We are cleansed,

And you are powerless.

We continue serving,

We rejoice that our names are written in heaven.

Great is the Lord.
Great is His faithfulness.
Great is His protection.
Now and always.
Amen.

Scripture Reference: Matthew 28:18, Luke 10:19, Deuteronomy 28:7

Prayer for Power over Darkness

We all go through unexplainable experiences when it seems there are invisible forces at work against us. The truth is, there might be. In those situations when what ails us cannot be seen by the naked eye, physical weapons do us no good. We must fight back with spiritual weaponry.

In chapter four of his New Testament book, Luke told the story of Jesus silencing a demon and casting it out of a man. We need to pray against demonic attacks toward us or others. Not everything negative is the result of demonic spirits. Some problems or issues could be consequences of our own actions or behaviors. Some circumstances are simply aspects of this world that threaten us. But some troubles and struggles are attacks from enemies in the spiritual realm. The apostle Paul wrote to the Ephesians that "our struggle is not against flesh and blood, but against the rulers, against the authorities, against the powers of this dark world and against the spiritual forces of evil in the heavenly realms" (Ephesians 6:12).

Whether the source of an attack on us (or others) is demonic or earthly, we need to call it out, acknowledge its influence, and ask God for victory over it.

Prayer

Almighty God,

The enemy is stalking, preying, and pouncing.

We can't save ourselves alone.

For the joy set before us,

Give us strength to endure and defeat.

Clothe us in Your armor.

Load our weapons with Your word.

By Your authority and power,

We admonish the oppressor within.

"Be quiet and be gone!" we rebuke sternly

The one that comes to kill and destroy.

For freedom, set us free,

To the amazement of all who see.

So none can then deny

That You are Lord of all.

Amen.

Scripture Reference: Hebrews 12:2, Ephesians 6:11-12, 2 Corinthians 10:4, Luke 4:35-37, John 10:10, Galatians 5:1

Prayer for Someone's Healing

Modern medicine is spectacularly effective. We can improve human health in miraculous ways that were impossible, even unfathomable just decades ago. However, who is at the source of medical phenomena? Is it doctors and researchers, or are medical advancements only possible because of the One who created us, the world, and everything natural in it?

Take the inexplicable ability of our bodies to heal themselves. God created our human flesh to restore itself after trauma and disease. We have the know-how and many resources to construct remedies that can rid our bodies of so many disorders. Yet, we were not built to last and live forever. Some maladies persist which neither our bodies nor medicine seem capable of overcoming. In such cases, we know God has the power to intervene. There are events recorded in scripture when Jesus told a sick person, "Your faith has made you well." Like medicine, faith can heal.

In prayers for healing, we can ask God to put His restorative hand on the sick, to touch the man-made treatment being administered, and to bolster the faith of the ill and their friends and family. And we can take all these examples from scriptural accounts to say, "God, You have done this before… Please do it again."

Prayer

Jehovah Rapha,

You are a God who heals.

Speak to these dry bones,

Breathe life into them,

And restore them to strength.

Cleanse this body,

Remove impurities that are hindering it,

Replace ailing cells with healthy tissue.

By faith,

Make this body well.

Give it peace,

And free it from suffering.

Amen.

Scripture Reference: Ezekiel 37:5-6, Luke 17:19, Luke 18:42, Mark 5:34, Luke 5:20

Prayer to Heal Many

We can pray for so many ailing people that we could spend hours, day after day, asking God to heal their health challenges. The number of people in our lives who seek restoration is overwhelming. We tell them one by one, "I'll be praying for you," but then days go by, and we get busy, forget, or learn of more people to pray for, and their names dissolve from our minds.

God knows what they need far better than we do. If we want to pray for all people who need healing, this is a prayer to cover every one of them. As you read this, open your mind to allow visions of the people for whom you pray.

Prayer

Jehovah Rapha,

Into Your healing hands

I lift every ailing soul that is on my heart.

You know their names and their circumstances.

You know what they need before I ask.

Reach out Your miraculous hand to them.

Whatever impedes them from receiving Your touch,

Remove it from their midst. Cleanse them.

Restore their bodies. Give them a hope and a future.

By their faith, or the faith of those who love them,

Make them well.

In the mighty and matchless name of Jesus.

Amen.

Scripture Reference: Exodus 15:26, Matthew 6:8, Jeremiah 29:11, Mark 5:34, Luke 5:20

Prayer to God the Provider

We all go through times when nothing is easy. Everything we do seems more complicated than it should be. We get hit with one challenge, obstacle, and resistance after another, with no end in sight. Remember that such times will pass. We have all been through them and have come out of them eventually.

So we look up and fix our eyes on the One who is Lord over all our circumstances. None of us will escape life's challenges, but God is Jehovah Jireh, the Lord who provides. He will give us everything we need to make it through.

Prayer

Jehovah Jireh,

So many people are hurting.

The challenges keep coming.

It seems the struggle is never-ending.

The enemy prowls around us like a roaring lion,

But he is an impostor.

You are the one true lion!

The Lion of Judah.

The King of kings,

And Lord of lords.

We take heart,

Because You have overcome the world.

Come quickly, Lord Jesus.

With a mighty hand and outstretched arm,

Subdue our adversaries.

Fortify our pathways.

Secure our footing.

Support our journey.

Lead us through,

To raise Your holy name

For all to see and know

That you are Provider, Protector, and Deliverer.
Amen.

Scripture Reference: Genesis 22:14, 1 Peter 5:8, Revelation 5:1-5, John 16:33, Psalm 136:12, Revelation 22:20

Prayer for Husbands and Wives

In his presidential farewell speech, Ronald Reagan said, "All great change in America begins at the dinner table." He meant that the foundation of a great nation is the family, the relationship between husbands and wives, and how parents raise their children.

Marriage and family have been under attack since the beginning of time, when Adam and Eve sinned in the Garden of Eden. This attack has been unrelenting, so we need to be even more unrelenting in our resolve to uphold strong, godly family values. The most significant and positive impact we can make is for husbands and wives to turn back to each other, turn to God together, and intentionally raise their children in godliness. We need to denounce the things that tear us apart, come to the dinner table, and reclaim our roles to restore our families and our nation.

Prayer

Almighty Lord,

Turn the hearts of husbands and wives to each other,

And their eyes toward You.

Have mercy on their children.

Look not upon the sins of their fathers.

Birth them again of the Spirit.

Cast out all evil from their homes.

Send hope to heal depression.

Send peace to suppress anger.

Send direction to guide the lost.

Pull them out of the pit.

Leave their darkness in the depth of the abyss.

Tell Your story on the pages of their future.

Amen.

Scripture Reference: Exodus 20:5, Ephesians 5:21, 25-29, 1 Peter 3:1-2

Prayer for the Youth

Spiritual revivals have historically begun with the youth of society. Perhaps it is because as we grow older, we become set in our ways, and young people are more energetic, generally seeking more fervently, and typically more curious about all aspects of life. What are we, as parents and mentors, teaching them to pursue? Are we turning their attention primarily to worldly aspirations or pointing them to God?

Throughout history, people groups, tribes, and nations have come to God, turned away, bore the consequences of walking apart from Him, and then returned to cry out for His presence. It is an undeniable cycle of God's people since the beginning of time. When it becomes clear that we are in that cycle, desperate for God's people to turn back to Him, look to the youth, pray for their protection, and ask God to use them to revive what has been lost.

Prayer

Abba, Father,
Raise the youth in this generation
To restore what once was Yours.
Claim Your children out of the hand of the enemy.
Ignite a flame of repentance.
Breathe the Holy Spirit into them,
And spread their fire across the land,
Into churches,
Across communities,
And settle it in our homes.
Here we are, Lord.
Start with us.
Revive our hearts.
Awaken Your people,
So that all will know You are the Lord.
Return to us as we return to You.
Blot out our sins,
That times of refreshing may come from Your presence.
Amen.

Scripture Reference: Psalm 85:6, Isaiah 6:8, Ephesians 5:14, Zechariah 1:3, Psalm 51:1

GLOBAL PRAYERS

Don't worry about anything; instead, pray about everything. Tell God what you need, and thank him for all he has done.

Philippians 4:6 NLT

In 1863, a few months past the halfway point of the Civil War in the United States, Abraham Lincoln issued a proclamation for "a day of Thanksgiving and Prayer to our beneficent Father who dwelleth in the heavens." He recommended that all citizens acknowledge God's blessings despite their transgressions; asked people to pray for those who mourned their loss; and "fervently" implored all to ask for God's "Almighty Hand to heal the wounds of the nation, and to restore it, as soon as may be consistent with the Divine purposes to the full enjoyment of peace, harmony, tranquility, and union."

What a humble and faithful prayer! Lincoln did not ask selfishly or for an immediate resolution to the war, but praised God for His grace and asked for healing and restoration as soon as it aligned to His will. Lincoln never witnessed the fullness of God's answer, having been assassinated just as the Civil War ended. The generations that followed, however, have been beneficiaries of God's response to that prayer for more than a century and a half.

The prophet Ezekiel gave a stirring word from God at the beginning of chapter 22 in his book, saying in verse 2, "Son of man, will you judge her? Will you judge this city of bloodshed?" Why does God declare judgment on these people? Because, as Ezekiel wrote in verse 30, "I looked for someone among them who would build up the wall and stand before me in the gap on behalf of the land so I would not have to destroy it, but I found no one." What does this mean? It means that our prayers can alter the future of nations. What a tremendous responsibility we have.

About 445 BC, Nehemiah, a Hebrew living in Persia and cupbearer to the king, learned of the great trouble the

Jewish remnant suffered after their exile and the desolation of Jerusalem. He wrote in Nehemiah 1:4, "When I heard these things, I sat down and wept. For some days, I mourned and fasted and prayed before the God of heaven." Nehemiah chapter 1 is a prayer in which he confesses the sins that the people of Israel have committed, reminds God of the promise He gave Moses to gather His people from exile, and asks God to grant him favor in returning to Jerusalem to rebuild the city. Nehemiah was asking God to use him to help fulfill the promise to all his people.

The psalmist wrote in Psalm 122:6-7, "Pray for the peace of Jerusalem: 'May those who love you be secure. May there be peace within your walls and security within your citadels.'" It was not only a request to pray over the people in Jerusalem during that time, but it is a prayer for all time, a prayer to impact all of human history.

In 1 Timothy 2:1-2, the apostle Paul urges, "That petitions, prayers, intercession and thanksgiving be made for all people—for kings and all those in authority, that we may live peaceful and quiet lives in all godliness and holiness." Why is Paul exhorting us to do this? He tells us in verses 3-4: "This is good, and pleases God our Savior, who wants all people to be saved and to come to a knowledge of the truth." Praying for people in positions of authority is essential for the well-being of those over whom they have dominion.

The most widely quoted scripture about praying for a nation is from 2 Chronicles 7. When King Solomon had finished building the Temple, the Lord appeared to him and said, "'I have heard your prayer and have chosen this place for myself as a temple for sacrifices.'" Take a moment to think about this from the perspective of a child. Is there anything more a child longs for than attention from a parent, to know that a parent is watching? "I have heard your prayer," God said. The child that still resides in all adults would delight to hear those words. Then God declares, "'If my people, who are called by my name, will humble themselves and pray and seek my face and turn from their wicked ways, then I will hear from heaven, and I will forgive their sin and will heal their land.'"

This passage contains four prerequisites. God says *if* we (1) humble ourselves, (2) pray, (3) seek Him, and (4) turn... *then* He will hear, forgive, and heal. Once again, we see not only how powerful but also how necessary prayer is in the healing of a nation or group of people.

When we have so much to pray for in our lives and over the people closest to us, it is easy to lose awareness that our prayers for nations and people groups are important. However, praying for our nation is just as powerful and effective.

Prayer Moment (Stephanie)

It was 2020 and cities in the United States were on fire. My husband is an Indiana State Trooper, and I feared for his life. It was hard to see him walk out the door every day, knowing that people wanted him dead for the uniform he wore and the badge on his chest.

My worries were not unfounded. Years earlier, on December 22, 2003, Scott Patrick, our friend, was shot and killed in the line of duty. He had stopped to help someone with a flat tire, not knowing that person was a convicted felon out on parole. Ever since that day, I knew the reality that, at any time, my husband might not make it home from work.

I spent many nights riddled with fear, certain I would hear the dreaded knock on the door and find a state trooper waiting to tell me my husband had been killed.

Living in fear is no way to live. Whether we're caught in a global pandemic, sending our loved ones off to war, or watching them walk out the door to protect citizens of the community, we can either pray and believe in the power of prayer, or we can worry. And when we worry, we tell God, "I do not trust You or believe You are in control."

I've been a police wife for 20 years, and yes, I still have thoughts about my husband not coming home. But I no longer sit and worry, wasting my life away, gripped by the unknown or fear of something that may never happen. I pray and give my husband over to God.

A sign hangs in our home, and it's a good reminder for us all: "The will of God will not take you where the grace of God will not protect you."

Prayer for Families

Many voices today argue about a lot of dissenting opinions on the role and construct of families. However, one thing is indisputable—the family unit's success is critical for a society's health and well-being. Decades of research show that, on average, married couples have better physical health, more financial stability, and greater social mobility.

Children of married couples are proven more likely to achieve higher academic performance and emotional maturity. Comparatively, children raised in single-parent homes are more likely to abuse drugs and alcohol, commit violent crimes, and drop out of school. Families are the bedrock of civilization.

While many in today's culture may be confused about the meaning and significance of a family, we can be sure that God is not confused. Therefore, scripture is the best place we can look to in prayer for our families. From scripture, we can ask God to reveal His purpose and to fulfill His will for families. We can ask Him to lead husbands, wives, and children in the way *He* wants them to go. As with any other supplication, we lay down our agenda, and accept His all-knowing, sovereign answers, convicted in our trust in Him.

Prayer

Heavenly Father,

If a house is divided against itself,

That house cannot stand.

I kneel before You,

The One from whom every family in heaven and on earth derives its name.

Out of Your glorious riches,

With the power of Your Spirit,

Strengthen families in their innermost being,

So that Christ will dwell in their hearts through faith.

Being rooted and established in love,

Give them the power to grasp how wide and long and high and deep is the love of Christ,

And to know this love that surpasses all knowledge.

Love that never fails.

Instill in husbands and wives the will to submit to one another out of reverence for Christ,

To love and respect each other as Christ loved the church.

Cover fathers with calm wisdom,

To raise their children in the training and instruction of the Lord,

So that when they are old, they will not depart from it.

Teach children to honor their parents,
So they may enjoy long life on the earth.
Raise voices to shout from the rooftops,
"As for me and my household,
We will serve the Lord."
Amen.

Scripture Reference: Mark 3:25, Ephesians 3:14-19, 1 Corinthians 13:8, Ephesians 6:4, Proverbs 22:6, Ephesians 6:2, Joshua 24:15

Prayer for the Military, First Responders, and Law Enforcement

The freedom we enjoy as Americans is largely dependent on protection provided by our military and law enforcement. Our freedom allows us to spread the gospel's good news more broadly. It allows for a greater opportunity to fulfill the Great Commission, sharing the message of Christ to all nations throughout the world.

In securing that freedom, first responders and law enforcement run *toward* danger to protect us *from* it. God bless them for that. The military is tasked with protecting our nation. Unfortunately, that duty often involves war and with war comes the loss of human life. Praying for the success of a military to win wars may seem contradictory to the mission of God's people.

On the other hand, war can be necessary to maintain freedom. Evil has no rules and will not stop. To align the purpose of our military with God's will, let us pray that the might of our armies are not used to serve human desire but to extend freedom, to allow the gospel to impact more people, and to usher more souls into the Kingdom of God. Let's pray for their protection to fulfill a divine purpose on earth.

Prayer

God of Heavenly Armies,

Strengthen our military, first responders, and law enforcement with Your mighty power.

Clothe them with Your full armor,

So they can take a stand against the devil's schemes.

Fix the belt of truth around their waist.

Cloak them with the breastplate of righteousness,

Fit their feet with the readiness that comes from the gospel of peace.

Give them a shield of faith to hold,

One that can extinguish all the flaming arrows of the evil one.

Cover them with the helmet of salvation,

And arm them with the sword of the Spirit.

Grant that the enemies who rise up are defeated before them.

Though they come at them from one direction, chase them away in seven.

Let all who rage against them be ashamed and disgraced,

Those who oppose them be as nothing and perish.

You are the Lord, take hold of their right hand,

And tell them, "Do not fear; I will help you."

Amen.

Scripture Reference: Ephesians 6:10-11, Deuteronomy 28:7, Isaiah 41:11-13

Prayer for Education

The educational system is a sizeable and vital segment of our culture. Students are in school from as young as two years old through their early to mid-twenties or beyond. It is a vulnerable time, when they are growing, physically and emotionally, more rapidly than at any other period of their lives.

Educators have a tremendous responsibility; however, we want God to spearhead our children's growth, enlightening students and teachers with His knowledge and wisdom. What good is it if students increase their knowledge, but none of it comes from a higher source and isn't developed to be used for a greater purpose? Within the lessons of mathematics, language arts, history, and more, let's ask God to anoint educators to impart His knowledge and for students to be open to receiving it.

Prayer

Almighty God,

See to it that no child is taken captive through hollow and deceptive philosophy.

Teach them to depend on Christ,

Rather than human tradition and the elemental spiritual forces of this world.

When they call out for insight and cry aloud for understanding,

Lead them to the fear of the Lord,

Impart Your knowledge upon them.

Anoint educators to teach Your instruction instead of worldly values,

Your knowledge, rather than the choice of gold,

Wisdom that is more precious than rubies.

Give them all the Spirit of wisdom and revelation,

So that they will know You better.

Amen.

Scripture Reference: Colossians 2:8, Proverbs 2:3-6, Proverbs 8:10-11, Ephesians 1:17

Prayer for the Church

What is the Church? Is it an organization? Is it a building? Is it a movement? However we define it, we should look to Jesus as its leader. He is the head of the Church. Human beings manage churches and run church organizations, so we need to fervently pray that the people in those positions are looking to Jesus as their boss, allowing Him to order their steps, and fulfilling His purpose in changing lives.

The church is not a perfect place of refuge; it is a spiritual hospital. It is to be available for emergencies, checkups, and maintenance, to take people in as they are and help them leave in greater spiritual health, more like Christ. Even today, disciples of Christ are aliens and strangers in the world, called to be salt and light, with a message of hope for all. Just as Jesus anointed His disciples and sent them out to teach, the church is responsible for positively influencing all corners of the world through the power of the gospel.

Prayer

Lord Jesus,

Image of the invisible God,

Firstborn over all creation.

You are before all things,

And in You, all things hold together.

You are the head of the body, the church.

Throw off everything that hinders,

And the sin that so easily entangles.

Fix our eyes on You,

The author and perfecter of our faith.

Build Your church upon the everlasting rock,

So the gates of hell will not overcome it.

As the Father and Son are one,

Unify Your church through their belief in You,

So the world will know that You love them.

Guard us against the pattern of this world,

And transform hearts by the renewing of minds.

Send us to where You are—

Give us the bread of life to feed the hungry,

Living water to quench the thirsty,

Shelter to welcome strangers,

Clothes to cover the naked,

Remedies to care for the sick,

Light to set prisoners free from darkness.

When pagans see the church, Your people, let them see You alone,

That they will glorify God

And grow in the grace and knowledge of the Lord Jesus Christ.

To Him be glory both now and forever!

Amen.

Scripture Reference: Colossians 1:15, Colossians 1:17-18, Hebrews 12:1-2, Matthew 16:18, John 17:23, Romans 12:2, Matthew 25:35-36, 1 Peter 2:12, 2 Peter 3:18

Prayer for Government

The government might be the most prominent social construct with divisive opinions, so much so that it appears most people have taken sides and are intent on working against each other. The uncomfortable reality is our government officials reflect *our* hearts. That is to say, their elevated status results from how we the people, living on Main Street in America, conduct our independent lives. Whether we vote for a particular officeholder or not, we are the influencers of our communities, and that influence raises those leaders to prominence.

We know we should pray for our leaders; however, it can be difficult to pray for leaders with whom we disagree; and, if we are willing to pray for them, it is tempting to pray that their plans fail. But who are we to say how God can use anyone in a leadership position? If God can take an evil, murderous man like Saul, and turn him into the apostle Paul, He can use anyone for His purpose. Let us pray for God to use whoever is in a position of authority (or any group of people) however He can to accomplish His will, that we can lead peaceful lives in all godliness and reverence of the one true King.

Prayer

Almighty God,

Consider this pledge,

And fulfill the promise of Your Word over our nation.

Blessed is the nation whose God is the Lord,

The people You chose for Your inheritance.

From heaven You look down and see all mankind;

From Your dwelling place You watch all who live on earth—

You, the One who forms the hearts of all,

Who considers everything we do.

Woe to those who make unjust laws,

To those who issue oppressive decrees,

To deprive the poor of their rights

And withhold justice from the oppressed of Your people,

Making widows their prey

And robbing the fatherless.

Give wisdom to kings,

Warn the rulers of the earth to serve You with fear

And celebrate Your rule with trembling.

For those who fear You,

Those whose hope is in Your unfailing love,

Deliver them from death and keep them alive in famine.

Praise be to Your name for ever and ever;

Wisdom and power are Yours.

You change times and seasons;

You depose kings and raise up others.

We wait in hope for You, Lord; You are our help and our shield.

In You our hearts rejoice, for we trust in Your holy name.

May Your unfailing love be with us, Lord, even as we put our hope in You.

Amen.

Scripture Reference: Psalm 33:12-15, Isaiah 10:1-2, Psalm 2:10-11, Psalm 33:18-19, Daniel 2:20-21, Psalm 33:20-22

Prayer for the United States of America

The hand of God has been on the United States of America from the time it was created until today. Without believing in God's guidance and favor, it is difficult to explain the great fortune and blessing bestowed upon one nation, and so rapidly. When considering how special America's existence is in the world, we should remember why and how she came into existence.

The idea came from a people seeking freedom to worship the God of the Bible freely and to see everyone as equal through the eyes of their Creator. Like any vast empire throughout history, such as the Roman and British, if America turns her back on God, she will also forfeit God's blessings. The pattern of those previous empires is clear. To continue in God's grace, a nation must be willing to persist in its allegiance to Him or return to Him if it has been led astray.

Prayer

Heavenly Father,

You called America into existence.

By Your mighty and merciful hand,

You have poured Your blessings upon her.

You have used her to be a beacon of light around the world.

Forgive us for turning away from You.

Look not upon our unfaithfulness,

But search from coast to coast,

Listening for the voice of Your children crying out for Your grace.

Save her once again.

Bless her to be a blessing.

Raise up Your voice of truth,

And set us free for Your purpose to prosper from within.

For Your honor and glory.

Amen.

Scripture Reference: Matthew 5:14, 2 Chronicles 16:9

Prayer for the Truth

What is truth? Pontius Pilate asked that question of Jesus, right before he handed Him over to be crucified. Three days later, the truth was revealed with the Lord's resurrection.

It feels like we are asking that same question today on a very regular basis. It is becoming increasingly difficult to ascertain what is true and what is false.

We need to look no further than the television news and talk shows. Turn on one channel and we will learn about an event; then, go to another channel and hear an opposite representation of the same event. How are we to know which is true? How do we determine truth from opinion?

Deception and distortion of the truth are rampant in our society. The uncertainty of not knowing what is real and who to believe is overwhelming and frightening. In Luke 8:17, it is written that "nothing is secret that will not be revealed, nor hidden that will not be known and come to light" (NKJV). A basis for prayer is that God will reveal His truth. When He does, we want to know how to discern it. We want to know, not only for our peace of mind but also for the peace of others and, most importantly, to have the ability to choose between good and evil, life and death, blessings and curses.

Prayer

Lord,

Truth has stumbled in the streets.

Honesty cannot enter.

Truth is nowhere to be found,

And whoever shuns evil becomes a prey.

Has the time come when people will not put up with sound doctrine?

Instead, to suit their own desires,

They gather around them a great number of teachers

To say what their itching ears want to hear.

They turn their ears away from the truth and turn aside to myths.

You made the earth,

You formed and established it.

We call to You,

Answer us,

And tell us the great and unsearchable things we do not know.

Disclose everything that is hidden.

Bring out into the open anything that is concealed.

If we hold to Your teaching, call us Your disciples,

That we will know the truth and walk in it.

By that truth, set us free.

Amen.

Scripture Reference: Isaiah 59:14-15, 2 Timothy 4:3-4, Jeremiah 33:2-3, John 8:31-32, Luke 8:17, 3 John 1:4

Prayer for Love

We request God to help us navigate this journey of life. We ask for strength, endurance, healing, direction, and countless other solutions to our trials and tribulations. Perhaps above all, love has the power to solve and conquer all our problems, challenges, struggles, and conflicts in life.

John said in 1 John 4:18, "There is no fear in love, but perfect love casts out fear" (NKJV). Peter wrote in 1 Peter 4:8 that "love covers over a multitude of sins." In the most widely known passage about love, Paul wrote a poetic description of it in 1 Corinthians 13; we hear it at wedding ceremonies. In that chapter, he declared, "Love never fails." If it never fails, perhaps we should also include a request for love in our prayers. It might be the ultimate resource and solution to all that ails us.

Prayer

Heavenly Father,
You are love.
Cleanse our iniquities
And the discord between us,
For love covers a multitude of sins.
Whoever seeks healing,
Bless with love.
In every home,
Clothe husbands and wives in love.
Comfort and protect children with Your love.
Wherever there is conflict and confusion,
Initiate love.
Shower us with patience, kindness, contentedness, and humility.
Cover us with honor, service, calm, and forgiveness.
Shine Your light of hope, truth, and protection ahead of us.
Instill perseverance on our hearts.
Thank you for the triumphs by Your love,
For love never fails.
Amen.

Scripture Reference: 1 John 4:8, 1 Corinthians 13:8, 1 Peter 4:8

AFTER PRAYERS

Listen to my voice in the morning, LORD. Each morning I bring my requests to you and wait expectantly.

Psalm 5:3 NLT

What To Do After We Pray

To officially mark the end of a prayer, we typically say, "Amen." It is how each prayer in this book is concluded. The word *Amen* essentially means "So be it." It is a declaration of belief, truth, and trust that what we say, request, or declare, is done. With "Amen," we acknowledge that what we said to God is, and will be, fulfilled.

However, our prayer work does not conclude when we say "Amen." There is a crucial component we must not forget, lest we risk forfeiting the full purpose of God's answer. That is, we must believe that God will answer our prayers as Jesus promised and, as best we can, remember what we have prayed for and about. Those two components go hand in hand, beginning with belief. If we believe, with convicted anticipation, that God will answer our prayers, we will be keenly alert to how and when He responds. However, if our belief is shallow, we are more likely to live with our eyes and ears muted to the handiwork of God around us. Belief fuels awareness.

When we ask God for something in prayer, James 1:6 tells us, "You must believe and not doubt, because the one who doubts is like a wave of the sea, blown and tossed by the wind."

Isn't that what it feels like to be in doubt? When uncertain if an outcome will be favorable, our thoughts tend to drift back and forth between positive and negative. Our emotions bounce around, as if tossed by the wind and the waves in a stormy sea. But James doesn't stop there. He continues in verses 7-8, "That person [who doubts] should not expect to receive anything from the Lord. Such a person is double-minded and unstable in all they do."

James spares no punches. He calls it as he sees it without care of hurting our feelings. Is he right? Should we expect nothing in return if we doubt God will answer our prayers? Are we double-minded and unstable?

Remember the conditional statement Jesus made in Mark 11:24, "'Whatever you ask for in prayer, *believe* that you have received it, and it will be yours.'" What we ask for in prayer will be ours *if* we believe. What does it say about our belief and trust in God if we forget what we pray about? Our doubt is greater than our belief when we continue worrying about what we voiced in our prayers. The worry manifests into fear. Fear leads us to actions that try to control outcomes. And we repeat that cycle throughout the day, until the time comes to pray again. Why would we worry if we prayed about it and trusted God completely? The answer is simple, and James points it out directly—we shouldn't worry, but we worry because we doubt.

Numerous accounts written in the Bible are evidence of God's response to prayer. Starting in the beginning, from Genesis 25:21, we are told that "Isaac prayed to the Lord on behalf of his wife, because she was childless. *The LORD answered his prayer*, and his wife Rebekah became pregnant." Ezra 8:23 says, "So we fasted and petitioned our God about this, and *he answered our prayer.*" Hebrews 5:7 tells us of Jesus, "He offered up prayers and petitions with fervent cries and tears to the one who could save him from death, *and he was heard* because of his reverent submission." (All italics are mine.) Throughout the Old and the New Testaments, prayer is mentioned over three hundred fifty times, often showing a response from God.

What should we do after we pray? We should watch and wait, being patiently aware. We don't want to watch so intently that we become exasperated or anxious. We need to be alert and awake to the promise that God will answer, in His perfect time, according to His perfect will.

Do prayers ever go unanswered? It may appear that way when we don't see an answer or if the answer is not what we had hoped. If we don't see God's response, we likely aren't paying enough attention to what He is doing. We said "Amen" and then dropped the prayers we had just prayed out of our consciousness. On the other hand, if God's response is opposite of what we asked of Him, it may seem He didn't listen or ignored us altogether. That happens more times than we would like, but when it does, perhaps God's answer was clearly "No." Whether it is "Yes" or "No," whether it comes in the way we expect or in a surprising way, God's answer should be more desirable than our desired outcome.

Sometimes, His answer is likely "Not yet." What do we do then? We remember, we watch, we wait. We show gratitude, we give thanks, we praise. And we keep praying.

Prayer Moment (Stephanie)

After pulling into a gravel driveway, we parked and exited our vehicle. I grabbed my husband's hand, and we trekked thirty-five wooded acres of our dream property. As I breathed in the cold air, puddles filled my eyes. I couldn't believe that in a few short months this property would be ours. I had prayed on more than one occasion that we would own enough land that I could walk out my back door and be on miles of trails. God had answered my prayers, or so I thought. We made an offer, and the seller accepted. Wahoo!

We put down our deposit and waited for the soil test results. Then the unexpected happened. The soil testing failed. We were surprised and devastated. But that devastation quickly turned to gratitude. Our realtor, wise enough to make the sale contingent on a soil test, protected us so we didn't waste thousands of dollars on unbuildable land.

Six months later, we "stumbled" upon a ten-acre wooded property with a home and a separate garage for my husband's woodworking projects. The house had not been updated since 1988. Another dream bubbled to the surface.

We had always wanted to remodel a house. We never envisioned it would be the home we were living in. We thought it would be a home we would buy and flip or use as a rental. God had other plans.

Once again, we made an offer, contingent on the home inspection. The home inspection revealed a litany of issues. The biggest? Mice overrunning the attic and insulation. Yikes! But sometimes major obstacles can be handled with the right expert. We made a couple of calls, and the rodent exterminators arrived and shared a plan we could execute. We moved forward.

Over the course of three months, we remodeled the entire home. Box springs with a mattress were set up in the living room. We had no kitchen, and I had the coffee pot in the laundry room. My jobs included hauling trim to the dumpster, removing wallpaper border, and scooting around on my hands and knees pulling staples out of the floor. I had not worked this hard ever before in my life. Every night I told myself that each of these tasks built mental strength.

I'm grateful for unanswered prayers. I can't fathom where we would be if we had purchased the thirty-five acres of bad soil. Sometimes God gives us what we need, not what we want.

BONUS PRAYER MOMENTS

BONUS PRAYER MOMENTS

Prayer Moment (Stephanie)

I wanted to keynote a Chamber of Commerce Women's Leadership Conference near my hometown, and I prayed for the opportunity. I reached out to the Executive Director, who told me they already had their speakers for the year. He asked that I reach out to him again in a few months. I was disappointed, but the door had not completely smacked shut in my face.

The following year, yours truly had been booked as the keynote speaker. I had an incredible day, the event went well, and I met wonderful women leaders. But what happened next made me realize that God often has bigger plans than we can see. Looking back, the real gift of the day was not the speaking opportunity. It was what happened after the event that would put everything into perspective.

After the event, I drove to a nearby nursing home facility. I walked into a room where one of my favorite teachers, Mrs. H, lay in bed, in the final days of her battle with ALS.

Tears streamed down my face as I held her hand. She lay frozen in bed, but her mind was clear as a mountain spring. She gave me a hard time about the colors of my outfit, as they were the colors of a rival school.

I could have sat there all day holding her hand. I can't describe the feeling, but I've never had someone hold my hand so intently, so connected. When another visitor entered the room, I didn't want to leave. I knew it would be the last time I'd ever see Mrs. H this side of heaven.

We kissed each other goodbye and exchanged I love yous. I tried to be strong but tears flowed without my permission.

As I walked out to my car, it hit me. The event was four hours from my home, and Mrs. H's nursing home was only minutes from the event. If I had gotten what I prayed for a year earlier, I would not have been in town to see Mrs. H in her last days. I'm still in awe of how God orchestrated my being in the right place at the right time to be with a person I loved dearly.

Anytime I get frustrated that a door I prayed to open is closed, I'm reminded that God sees a picture we don't see. And even when we don't see it, He always has the perfect plan for our life. We must trust and believe.

Prayer Moment (Stephanie)

Do you have days when you forget the prayers God has answered in your life?

Sometimes in life, we hit a stretch when nothing seems to be going our way.

I like writing down my prayers. A college friend gave me the idea when I shared with him that I'd often get lost in thought or distracted when praying. He recommended I write down my prayers, which would help me focus. Twenty-five years later, I'm still writing them down.

Writing down my prayers keeps me focused, and I love going back, reading my requests, and noting when God answered them. Many of these answered prayers turn into what I'm thankful for; I get to see and remember how God is working in my life and the lives of others. Documenting the prayers God answers is helpful when we don't feel like He's heard our current prayers or isn't answering how we think He should.

Here is one prayer I pray often: "Lord, protect me. Give me strength. Take away my fear. Please let me go to sleep and stay asleep."

In high school, I attended a concert with a friend. When he dropped me off at home, my parents were not there. I let myself in the house, went to my room, and passed out.

The next morning, rays of light streamed into the room, and I wondered why my blinds were open. I knew they had been closed when I left for the concert. Sauntering into the living room, I asked my mom why she'd opened my blinds.

"I didn't. We need to chat." My mom's serious response concerned me.

I won't go into all the details, but the gist of the story is the police believe a stranger had been in the house when I came home and had entered my room while I slept. By the grace of God, I never woke up through the entire ordeal.

Though I was physically unharmed, that one event wrecked me emotionally and changed my perspective on life and my sense of security. Twenty-five years later, I struggle when I'm home alone and often live in fear.

Anxiety pours over me like a crashing waterfall when my husband isn't home in the evenings or is away on a work trip. Sometimes, I still have anxiety when he is lying beside me in bed.

But not every night is a struggle. Here is an entry from my journal on April 2, 2017:

"Mike was at the lake house. I always stay up until I'm completely exhausted. Right before I go to sleep, I ask God to give me protection and to sleep through the night. This morning I woke up at 7:00 a.m. I never sleep this late. God is good."

Every time I read this entry, I'm reminded that not all nights when my husband is gone are bad. I *can* have a good night's sleep.

God may not answer all our prayers; but when He does, take note and be grateful.

Prayer Moment (Mike)

The average person will work approximately one hundred thousand hours in a lifetime. That is over twenty percent of our awake time. Yet so few of us think to include our jobs, the companies we work for, and the people we work with in our prayers.

Whenever people ask for prayer over a job-related circumstance, it is usually about an interview they have or a particular problem at their company. Rarely do we hear of people praying for a company itself, for its mission to be lived out in a godly and meaningful way, and for the employees to fulfill their part in achieving that mission. As with any other aspect of our lives, our work comes with its fair share of challenges. If the job serves a worthy cause, why would we not ask the most powerful force in the universe for help in carrying it out?

One day, I realized that I rarely prayed for God to help guide the companies I had worked for. I asked a few co-workers what they thought of meeting to pray. They all agreed it would be great to pray together. We gathered each week for a few minutes to ask God to help the company overall with the service it provided—a noble vision of improving the quality of life for as many people as possible. We said prayers for our projects, individual pursuits, and each other.

As the demands for our service increased and our individual and collective workloads multiplied over time, God showed up and let us know He was listening and sending assistance. I often asked God very directly for more time. I pleaded with Him to create time. We all know there are twenty-four hours in a day and seven days in a week, but God doesn't measure time like us. Peter wrote in 2 Peter 3:8, "Do not forget this one thing, dear friends: With the Lord, a day is like a thousand years, and a thousand years are like a day."

I didn't know how He could create time, but I asked anyway. Somehow, I believed He could expand the day's twenty-four hours into twenty-five, twenty-six, or more. Wouldn't you know it, on multiple occasions, I arrived at my desk after the group prayer, opened my email, and received meeting cancellations that opened blocks of time on my calendar. This happened more than once, and it was never by my own inducement. I asked God to do the impossible, and He did. He created time.

The years following the beginning of our prayer group were some of the most challenging in the history of our industry. Financial pressures weighed on many other businesses like ours, leading some to close their doors and others to downsize considerably. Throughout that time, our company thrived. Its mission was expanded from a foundation of financial stability that was as strong as ever. Was that success a result of God answering the prayers of our little group each week? You can decide for yourself. As for me, I will keep praying!

Prayer Moment (Stephanie)

When I travel, I pray point to point. What does that mean? I'll give you an example. I recently flew to Austin, Texas. I prayed from my home to the Midway Airport, from Midway Airport to the Austin Airport, from the Austin Airport to my hotel, from my hotel to the event (and back), from the hotel to the Austin Airport, from the Austin Airport back to the Midway Airport, and from the Midway Airport to home.

This may seem a bit laborious, but it gives me great comfort to know that I have asked God to protect me each step of the way.

Prayer Moment (Mike)

"My little girl has cancer," were concerned words by a good friend from church. His daughter was in preschool and had been diagnosed with leukemia. Her long-term prognosis was unknown. She had a series of treatments and a long road ahead until an outcome could be understood. While she was in the physical care of her doctors, our family and countless other families went to work in prayer. We started the prayer journey for this precious girl—and it was a journey—by gathering a few families to pray over her, over the family's house, yard, and everything she would be surrounded by as she began her battle.

My kids were in elementary school at the time. Our family had recently gotten into a nightly routine of praying together before bedtime, so we added this special girl to our prayers. We prayed for her almost every night for the next several years, which is not an exaggeration. That is how long it took for us to see God's hand at work and His ultimate answers. We watched, persisted, and remained patient. Today, that little girl, who endured more physical and emotional challenges than most people will in their lifetime, is in high school and is cancer free.

Would the outcome of her health have been different without the thousands of prayers for her over the years? We don't know. If we had stopped praying during that time, would God still have healed her? Again, we don't know. However, we do know from the book of Daniel chapter 10 that Daniel prayed for three weeks. After the third week, he was visited by an angel who said to him, "'Since the first day that you set your mind to gain understanding and to humble yourself before your God, your words were heard, and I have come in response to them. But the prince of the Persian kingdom resisted me twenty-one days. Then Michael, one of the chief princes, came to help me, because I was detained there with the king of Persia'" (verses 12-13). Had Daniel ceased praying before the twenty-first day, would Michael have had the power to help the angel escape? Would the angel have still been delivered to answer Daniel's persistent prayers? Though it is not clear, it is possible that Daniel's persistence in prayer unleashed the power to deliver an answer. Likewise, so can ours.

When You Don't Know What or Who To Pray For

I (Stephanie) don't know about you, but sometimes I sit down to pray, and my mind is blank. Maybe I'm weary, just waking up, or feeling down and out.

During these times, I listen to what God says to me.

For my prayer and gratitude journal, *Thank-You Notes to God*, I compiled a list of things we can always pray for as we chat with God.

Make these topics specific to the calling of your heart.

Can you imagine how our world would change if every believer prayed for these things?

Pray for:

- the hopeless
- those going through trials
- protection of our men and women in the military
- salvation of nonbelievers
- those engaged in spiritual warfare
- women and children trapped in abusive relationships
- victims of sexual assault
- those in the bondage of sin
- drug addicts
- the oppressed
- churches

- injustices in our society
- children who are bullied in school
- families in financial crisis
- the homeless
- those who are lonely
- couples struggling with infertility
- single people who long for a lifelong partner
- marriages
- guidance and direction in life (ourselves and others)
- our enemies
- cancer patients
- healthcare workers
- police officers for both their physical and mental well-being
- those who are grieving the loss of a loved one
- children who have strayed away from their parents and homes
- missing children
- people we need to forgive
- prisoners in our correctional facilities and the staff who care for them
- pastors and church staff
- community and nonprofit organizations

- our president, vice president, Congress, and the Supreme Court
- our country
- countries around the world
- farmers and abundant crops
- encouragement for those who need it
- financial troubles
- faith when we have doubts
- courage when we are fearful
- rest for a weary soul
- dependence on the Lord
- discernment of what is true and not true, good versus evil
- addictions to food, sugar, and alcohol
- doors of opportunity to open
- small businesses
- a deeper, stronger faith
- a joyful heart
- contentment with what I have and where I am in life
- my spouse
- my children
- my extended family

- my friends
- strangers that cross my path
- college students
- courage to share the love of Jesus Christ
- peace in our world
- the hungry to be fed and provided with clean water
- healing for diseases
- medical breakthroughs
- a good night's sleep
- the ability to say no to the activities that are not serving the Lord
- the courage to quit "busy"
- an attitude of gratitude
- a generous heart
- eyes to see people like Christ Jesus does
- anger in my heart to dissipate
- a deeper faith
- humility
- safe travels

Let's Stay Connected!

We would love to connect with you:

Mike Bellini

www.mikebellini.com

Instagram @MikeBellini_

Podcast: The Ultra Marriage Podcast

Email: mike@mikebellini.com

Stephanie L. Jones

www.givingyourbestlife.com

Email: stephanie@givinggal.com

Instagram @Giving_Gal

Facebook @GivingGal

Podcast: Giving Your Best Life

Children's Books: www.givinggalbooks.com

APPENDIX

Prayer	Page
America	140
Belief in the Unseen	58
Called for His Purpose	31
Clarity	60
Clean Heart	29
Combating Evil	33
Confession	19
Direction and Guidance	85
Education	132
Embracing Discomfort	68
Face the Storm	70
Families	126
Freedom from Worry	66
God the Provider	114
Government	137
Gratitude in Adversity	77
Healing for a Person	110
Healing for Many	112
Help in any Situation	88
How God Sees Me	75
Humility	27

Husbands and Wives..117
Lengthy Struggle...35
Love...145
Military & First Responders............................129
Perspective..52
Power over Darkness..108
Prepare for the Lord..92
Pride...73
Protecting Your Home......................................105
Protection..22
Purpose and Direction......................................46
Repentance..64
Restless Desire..98
Search for Meaning...49
Seeking God..54
Spiritual Sight...56
Spiritual Warfare...25
Successful Outcomes..94
Thankfulness...79
The Church...134
The Lord's Blessing..90
The Lord's Prayer...16
Travel Guidance..96

UNCOMMON PRAYERS

Trust and Obedience..62
Truth...142
Youth..119

ACKNOWLEDGMENTS

Yeshua, there is no power of prayer without You. Thank you for being our great high priest, allowing us to approach the Father's throne of grace with confidence and authority, able to receive mercy and find grace to help us in our time of need.

Cindy and Jonathan, thank you for giving your hearts, time, and valuable feedback in being the first to read the early draft of this book. It would not have become what it is without you.

Our editor, Elaine Starner. As always, it was a pleasure working with you. Thanks for making our book better.

Our readers, faithful followers, family, and friends. Thank you from the bottom of our hearts for all your love, support, and big cheers from the sidelines. We can't do this work without you!

OTHER BOOKS BY THE AUTHORS